EASY ROCK BASS

BY DIETER PETEREIT
CD INCLUDED

TABULATURE
MUSIC NOTATION
EXERCISES
TECHNIQUES

MORE THAN **50** LICKS

FUNK
SOUL
REGGAE
POP
ROCK

Voggenreiter

No part of this publication, such as the music, text, design or graphics, may be reproduced in any form or by any means without the prior written permission of the publishers.

Cover design by: OZ, Essen (Christian Brackmann & Katrin Nacke)

VOGGENREITER PUBLISHERS
P. O. Box 210126, 53156 Bonn/Germany
www.voggenreiter.de
info@voggenreiter.de

© 1988 by Voggenreiter Publishers
International Copyright Secured
All Rights Reserved
ISBN: 3-8024-0173-5

Preface

This book seeks to show all the main functions of the bass guitar. It shows you the important techniques and examples to help you start your bass career in a short period of time. If you wish, you can use the easy-to-read TAB system, showing you the exact fretting position in each example.
Many examples in this book are also played on the CD, which makes everything much clearer. With those three little helpers, and the other hints and tips in this book, you almost can't go wrong.
I'm sure you'll "get the groove" pretty soon and will continually enjoy the versatility of this instrument.

On this note...

Content

Chapter 1 7

The Bass Guitar 8
Stringing Your Bass 10
Tuning 12
Sounds and Amplification 14
Playing Positions 15
Playing with a Pick 18

Chapter 2 19

Blues with the Metronome 20
The Basics 23
Let's Go, but: IN TIME 28
Blues with Half Notes 30
Rock Blues 32
Blues in A with Half and Quarter Notes 36
Blues in A with Quarter and Eighth Notes 38
Blues in A with Eighth Notes 40
Blues-Solo in A 42
Fast Rock 43

Chapter 3 45

The "Stress-String" 46
"Land Drill" 48
Blues 50
The Key of C major 55
Walking Bass 57
Rhythm and Blues 59
The House of the Rising Sun 61
Harmony 65

Chapter 4 69

Soul Music	70
Soulbrothers Delight	76
Memphis Soul	78
Rhythm & Blues	79
Otis Blue	80
Mustang Annie	81
Alternating Bass Notes	82
Triad's Rock	84
Shuffle	87
Shuffle Blues	88
Heavy Rock Shuffle	90
Wave Rock Licks	93

Chapter 5 95

Classical Pop	99
Bonding Notes	100
Double stops in 10ths	101
Double stops in 5ths	102
Double stops in Major 7ths	104
Double stops in Minor 7ths	105
Funk is Fun	106
Fill-ins (in 8ths and 16ths)	108
Fun(k) Licks	112
More Funk	113
Motown Shuffle 1	117
Motown Shuffle 2	118
Motown Shuffle 3	119
Motown Shuffle 4	120
Rastaman Reggae	121
More Reggae	122

Chapter 6 125

Slap Bass Technique 126
String "Popping" 132
Dead Notes 134
Slap + Pop + Dead 137
Hammer-Ons 138
Pull-Offs 140
Slap + Pop + Dead Notes + H/O + P/O 141
CD Playlist 142

Chapter 1

The Bass Guitar

... and what you should consider, when making your choice.

There's a wide variety of new and used basses on the market, and I'm sure there's one that perfectly suits you. Do not decide on a bass guitar just because it may look hot and make sure you ask a more advanced fellow bass player or a salesman for advice.
A large amount of technical features does not necessarily make a better quality bass. There are basses that are packed with new electronics and hardware. They may look pretty impressive, but these features often only conceal real insufficiencies of the instrument. A simple, used instrument is often a better choice than a fancy, super bass. Of course, another factor is the price of such an instrument, but I'd prefer a basic, used bass to a new, high-end weapon. If you watch the bass scene for a while, you will see many popular bass players using the same bass guitars everywhere around the world. This doesn't mean that this type of human being is more conservative than others, but these bass guitars work in all positions. You can change some components as you progress, but the basics (i.e., neck + body/fretboard) have to be right. In other words: it's better to distinguish between good features and useless ones, than giving preferene to a new guitar over an old one.

The same goes for the shape of the instrument and your seated playing position. Try using the bass with a strap that's comfortable to you (do not use a strap that's too slim, but also avoid ones that are too wide, because they tend to hurt your neck). If the neck of your bass "pulls downward" when you play while standing, it is too heavy and you will have to correct your playing position all the time. I recommend you not to buy such an instrument and to choose some other bass guitar instead. The same goes for bass guitars whose necks "pull upward". There are some bass shapes that have proven themselves over time. Try which ones "suit you best" by comparing the individual models. Also, watch the weight of your new bass guitar. Some basses weigh so much that your back aches after only a few minutes. The weight depends on the wood type and hardware that's being used and, of course, the size of the body. I recommend you not to burden yourself irrationally. A slim neck and a medium width fretboard are appropriate for the beginner with smaller hands.
The fretboard and the access (string-to-fretboard distance) should allow you to fret the strings without having to use too much power. The string access is normally adjustable. You can adjust the access either on the string trees located on the bridge or, alternatively, in most cases you can also alter the string access by adjusting the neck tilt at the top or bottom of the fretboard. But be careful: do not break it. Make sure you have an expert adjust your bass, as this is almost a science by itself. Bass strings are available in different gauges. Different gauges cause different tension on the neck. For instance, if you use a heavier gauge, you increase the tension, which results in raising the access. In this case, you will have to lower the access again. Let a bass "authority" show you how this works.

Let's take a look at the visible parts of your "new love":

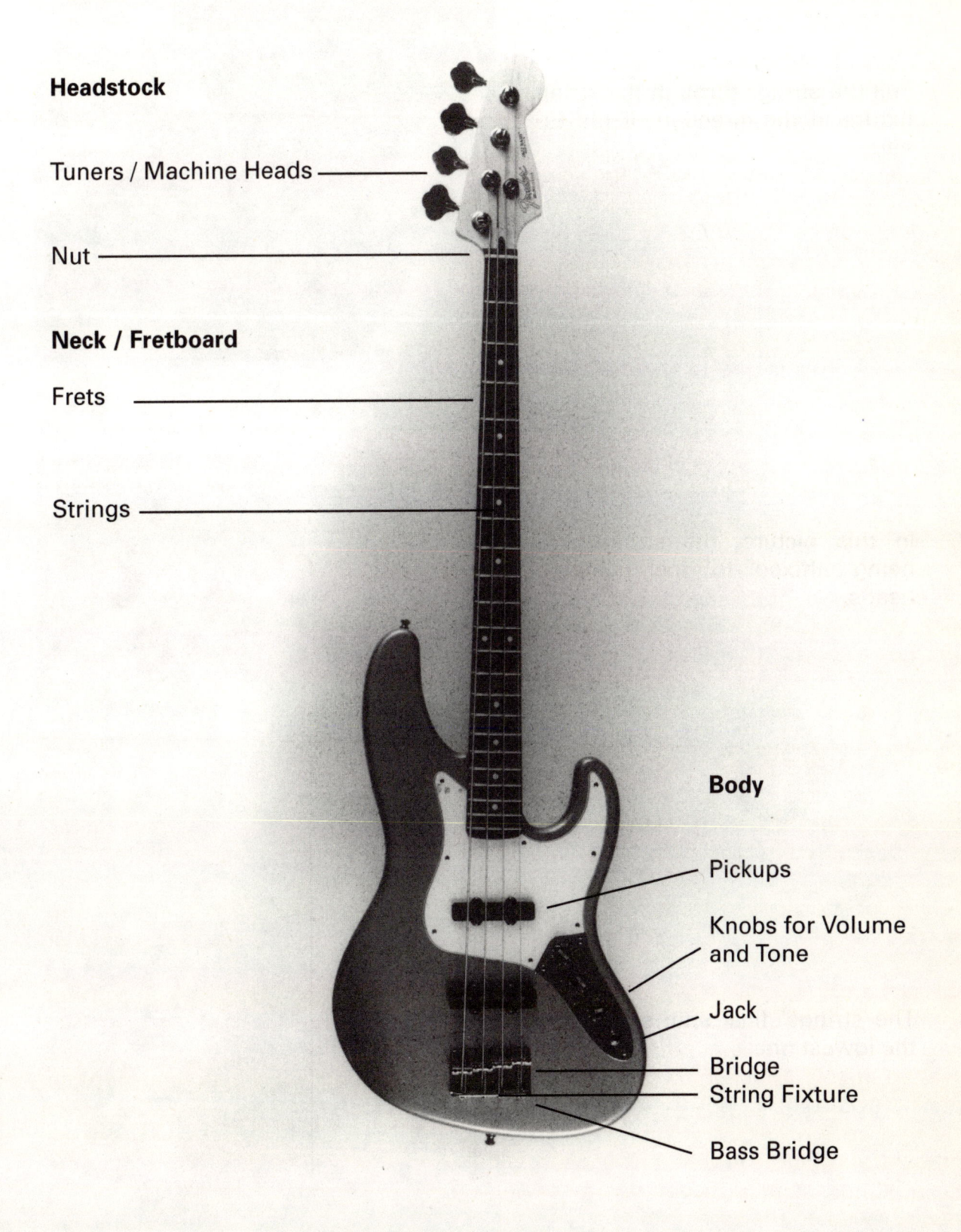

Headstock

Tuners / Machine Heads

Nut

Neck / Fretboard

Frets

Strings

Body

Pickups

Knobs for Volume and Tone

Jack

Bridge
String Fixture

Bass Bridge

9

Stringing Your Bass

1. Pull the strings through the string fixture in the direction of the tuners.

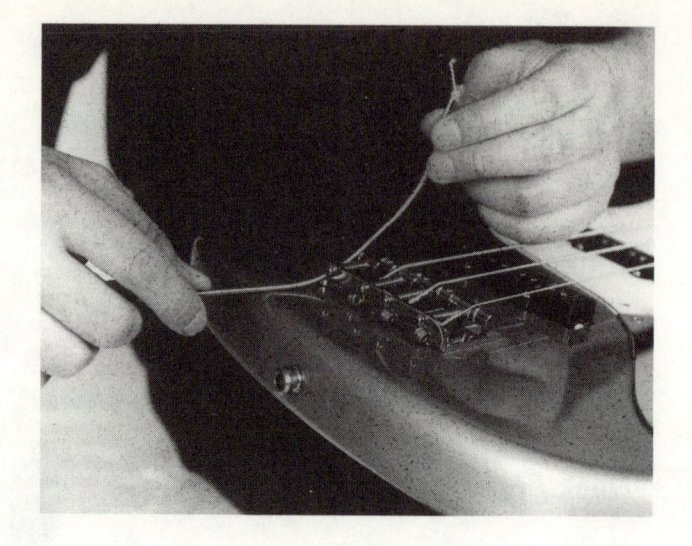

2. In this picture, the strings are being affixed to the machine heads.

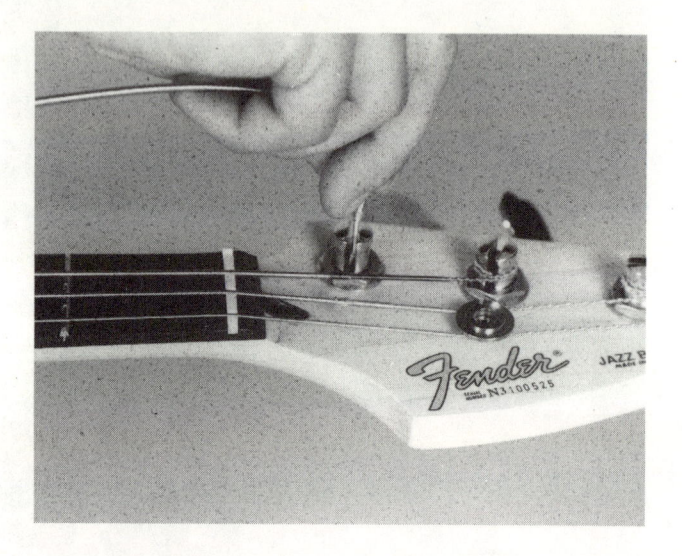

3. The strings' final spin should be the lowest one.

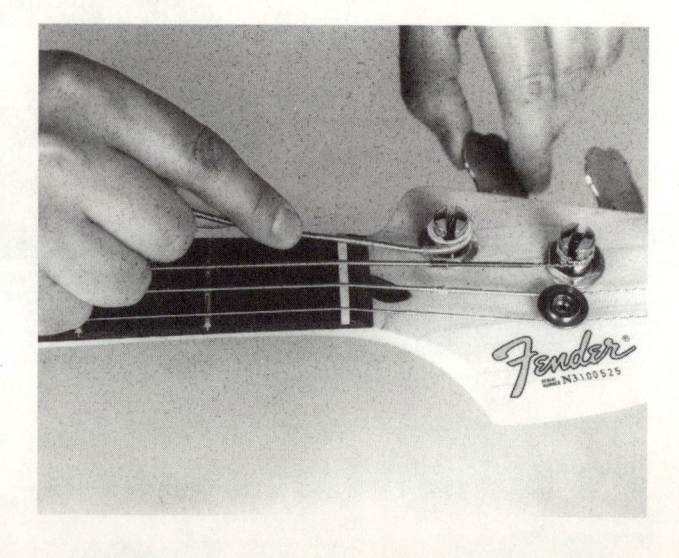

4. This is how you tighten the tuners. Turn the tuners more carefully when the strings feel tight. On the next page I'll tell you which string goes where and how to tune up.

5. Make sure that the strings are resting in the notches of the bridge and nut.

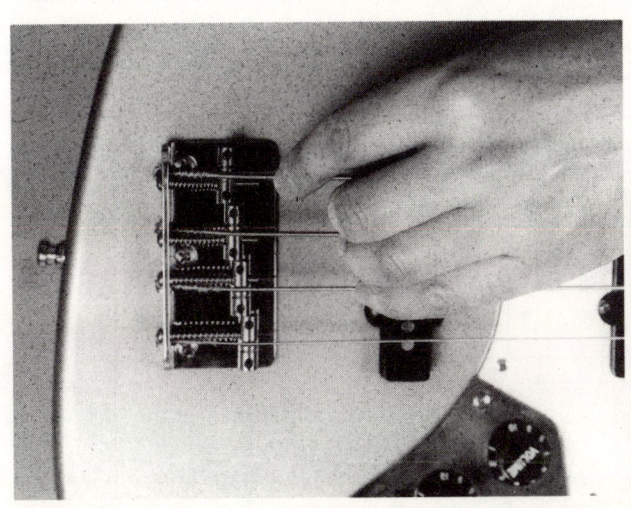

7. Some basses have additional string guiding which helps to keep the string down.

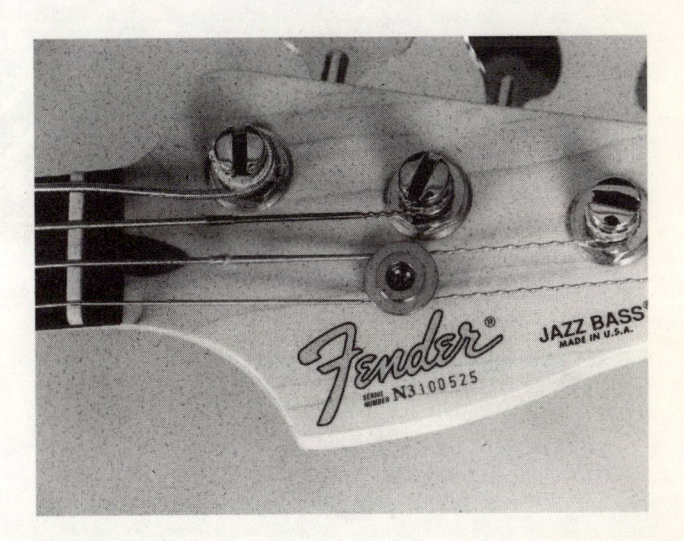

11

Tuning Up

Before you start playing, you need to tune your bass.
Here's how it works:

First you have to know the names of the notes of the strings:

First string: G (the thinnest string is the highest one)
Second string: D
Third string: A
Fourth string: E (the thickest string is the lowest one)

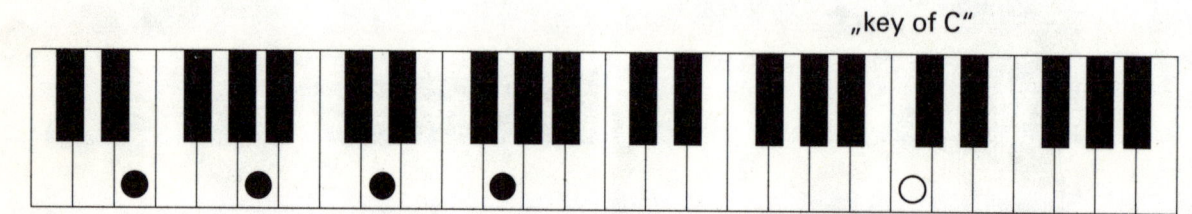

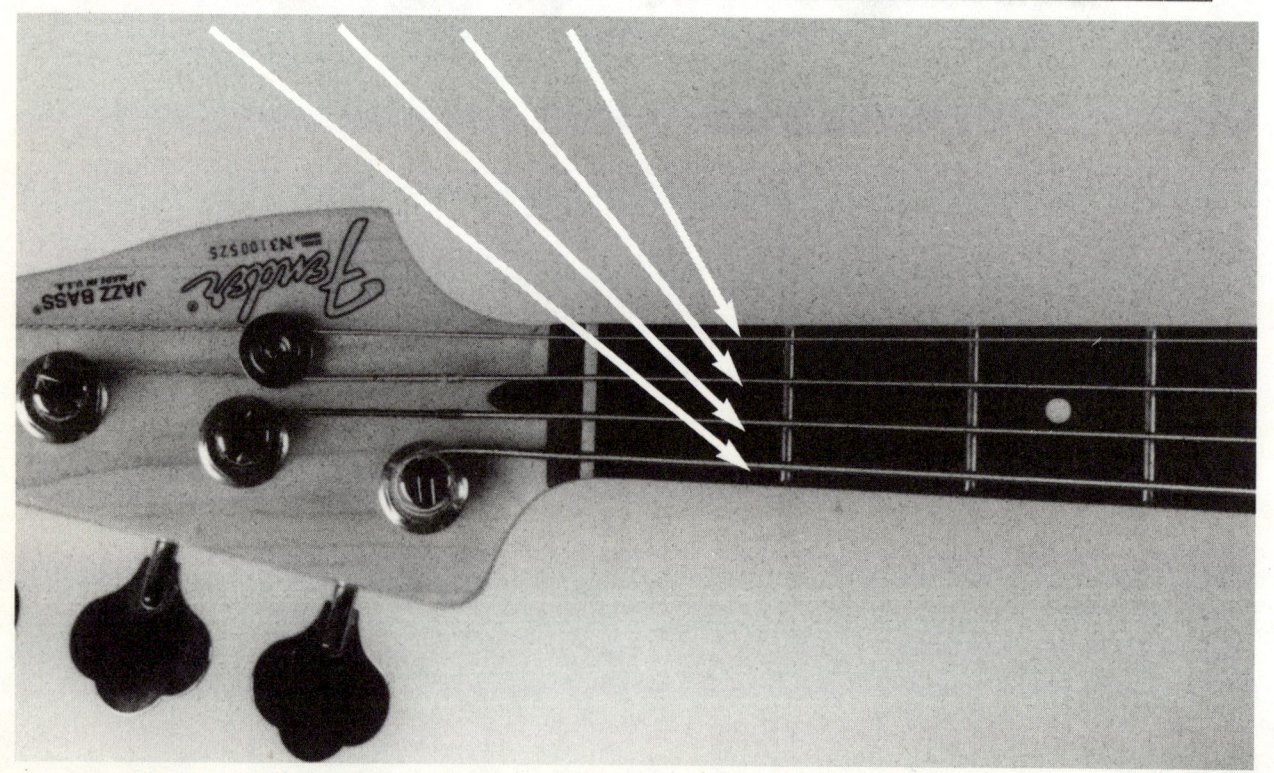

"key of C"

TAKE 1

Now, put in the CD.
In the first example (TAKE 1), the notes of each string are given. Listen to the notes and then tighten the string by slowly turning the tuner until the string sounds right.
If you now hit the open strings you get the notes: G - D - A - E.

In case you have a piano at your disposal, you can also use it as a reference for tuning your bass. You'll find the right notes on the previous page.

By the way: electronic tuning devices with displays are available, which help you tune your instrument very accurately. But go ahead and train your ears first!

The notes of a tuned bass look like this in standard notation:

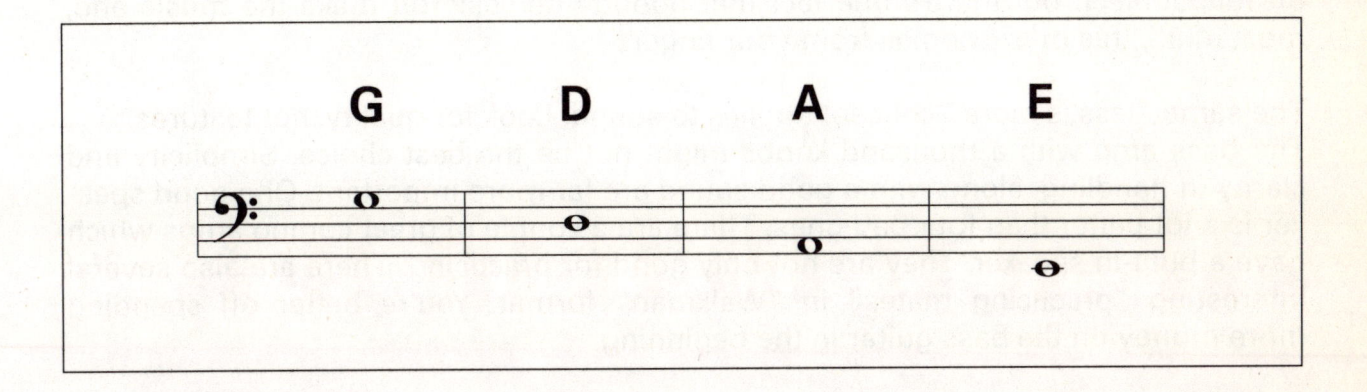

In standard notation, one note is assigned to each line and space. The names of the notes also depend on the clef at the beginning of the line. In this case, we're using the bass clef. The two dots indicate that the note F is located on the second line. From there, you can start counting up and down the other notes.

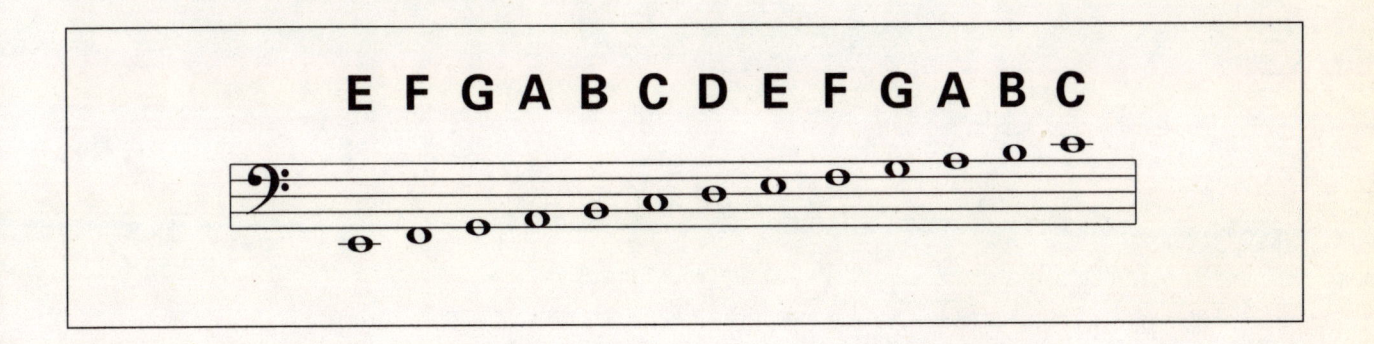

Your Sound

... and what it takes

The sound of your instrument depends on several factors which sometimes interact with each other. Basses vary in tone, depending on the wood from which they are made. A finished maple neck sounds different to one made of ebony. A body made of graphite will sound different to a plywood body built from several different types of exotic wood. Pickups, pre amps, amplifiers, speakers and so forth all feature different sounds, aside from the endless possibilities offered by effect units. But most of all, your playing technique will have a major impact on "your sound".

There's a vast number of musicians' magazines out there and even more opinions on this subject, but there's one fact that nobody denies: You make the music and, most of all, this music comes from your fingers.

The same "less is more" concept applies to sound. Look for quality, not features.
The bass amp with a thousand knobs might not be the best choice. Simplicity and clarity in handling, along with a good sound are far more important. One good speaker is a lot better than four bad ones. There are a couple of great combo amps which have a built-in speaker. They are not only good for practicing. There are also several interesting "practicing mates" in "Walkman" format. You're better off spending more money on the bass guitar in the beginning.

Another factor are the strings you are using. Round wound strings produce more sustain than flat-wound ones. Flat wounds are easier on the skin of your fingertips. I recommend medium-gauge strings in the beginning.

Playing Positions

In the seated position, your right forearm rests on the body of the bass ...

as it also does in the standing position:

Left Hand

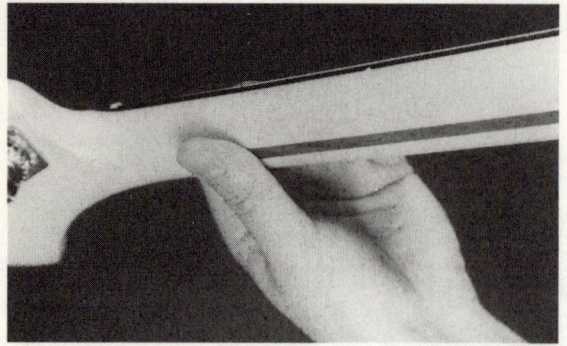

Place your thumb mid way along the rear side of the fretboard - more or less the thickest part of the neck.

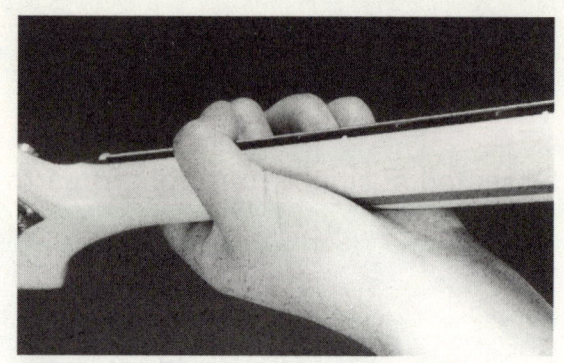

Your thumb should not cross over the borders of the fretboard. Not only does it look odd, it also limits the precision and strength of your playing.

Your hand should bend over the strings in the form of an arch, in order to ensure proper pressure on the strings.

With your fingers bent backwards, accurate fretting is impossible.

This also applies to fingers sticking out over the fretboard.

Here's an example of the optimum playing position. The center of your fingertips press the strings onto the fretboard.

Hint: Your fingernails should be cut short, in order to ensure accurate fretting.

Right Hand

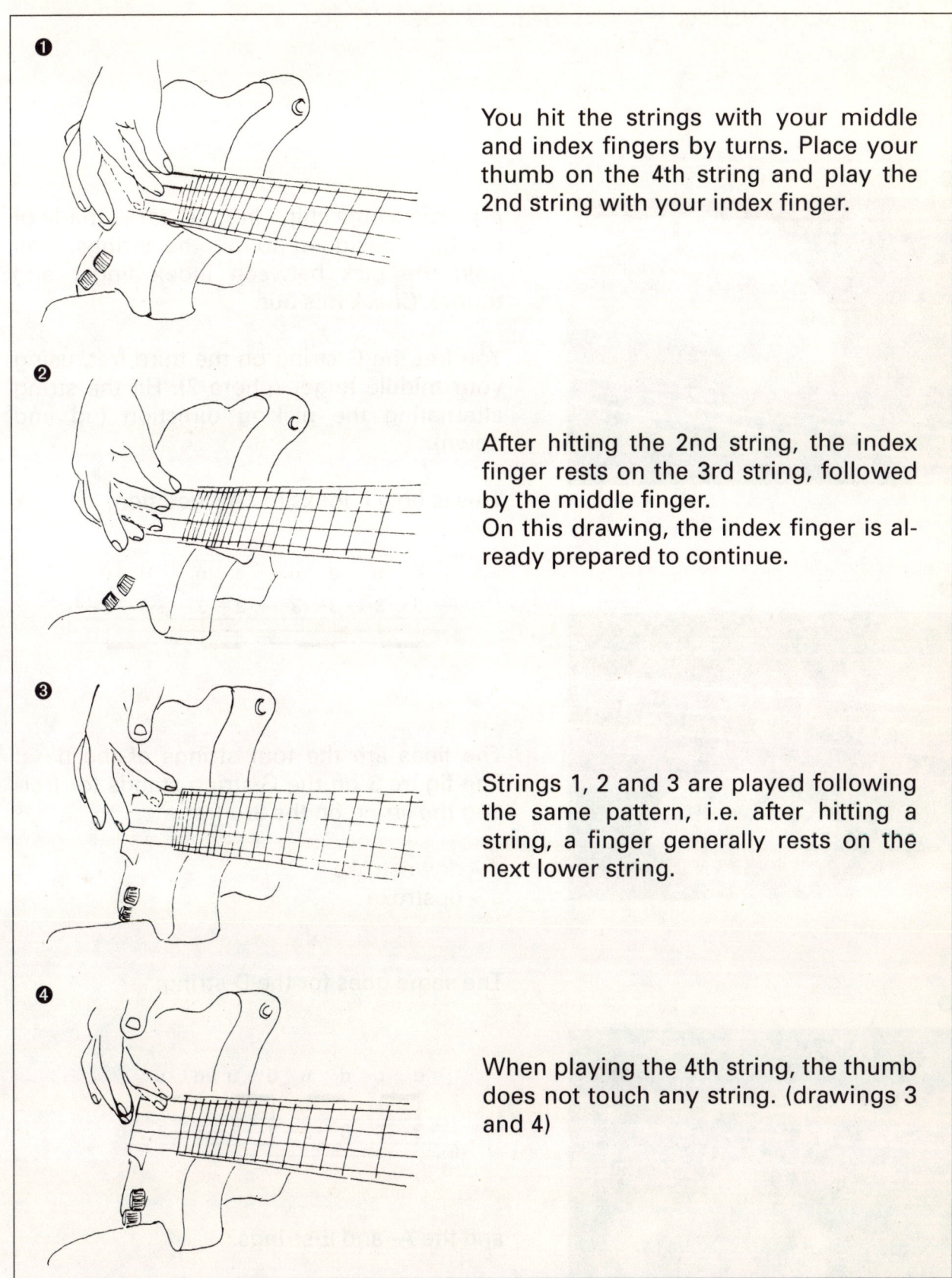

❶ You hit the strings with your middle and index fingers by turns. Place your thumb on the 4th string and play the 2nd string with your index finger.

❷ After hitting the 2nd string, the index finger rests on the 3rd string, followed by the middle finger.
On this drawing, the index finger is already prepared to continue.

❸ Strings 1, 2 and 3 are played following the same pattern, i.e. after hitting a string, a finger generally rests on the next lower string.

❹ When playing the 4th string, the thumb does not touch any string. (drawings 3 and 4)

The sound changes because of the different playing positions of your right hand. The closer to the fretboard you hit the strings, the more substantial and the warmer the sound gets. Hitting the strings closer to the bridge leads to a thinner sound. Check it out yourself!

Playing with a Pick

❶

A pick is a little chip - in most cases made of plastic - designed to hit the strings. You hold the pick between index finger and thumb. Check this out:

You fret the G-string on the third fret, using your middle finger (photo 2). Hit the string alternating the picking direction (up and down).

This is how it looks in TAB notation:

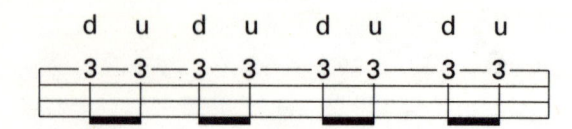

```
    d   u   d   u     d   u   d   u
 ─3─── 3─── 3─── 3────3─── 3─── 3─── 3─
```

❷

The lines are the four strings of the bass. The figure 3 on the G-string stands for fretting the string on the 3rd fret.

d = downstroke
u = upstroke

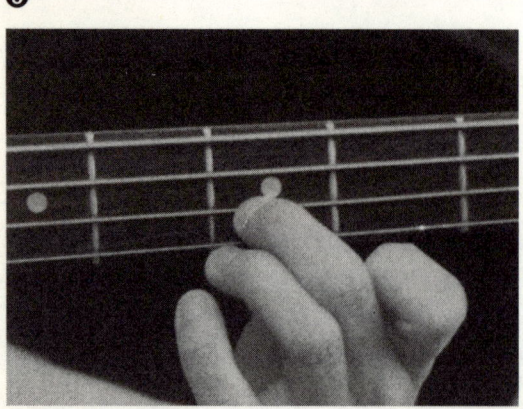

The same goes for the D-string:

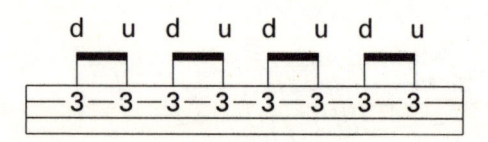

```
    d   u   d   u   d   u   d   u
 ─3─── 3─── 3─── 3─── 3─── 3─── 3─── 3─
```

❸

and the A- and E-strings.

18

Chapter 2

Blues with the Metronome

Listen to Take 2 on the CD. You'll hear steady clicks. Those are the beats of a "metronome" (a mechanical timekeeper), helping us to keep the rhythm.

Take your bass guitar, count off 1 - 2 - 3 - 4, and then you hit the open E-string, i.e., you play it like it is, without fretting anywhere on the fretboard.

TAKE 2

	bar 1	bar 2	bar 3	bar 4
1-2-3-4	E E E E 1 2 3 4	E E E E 1 2 3 4	E E E E 1 2 3 4	E E E E 1 2 3 4

▲ Start playing from here. Count out loud.

In standard notation what you've played looks like this:

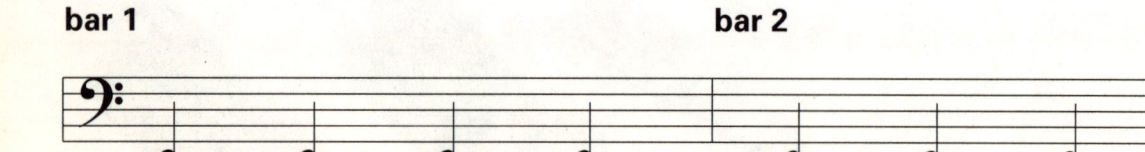

bar 1   bar 2

𝄢   ●   ●   ●   ●   ●   ●   ●   ●
    1   2   3   4   1   2   3   4

bar 3   bar 4

𝄢   ●   ●   ●   ●   ●   ●   ●   ●
    1   2   3   4   1   2   3   4

All right? Cool, let's continue with your first real song!

For the following twelve bar pattern you are playing on the A, D, and G-strings. Count 1 - 2 - 3 - 4 again, and here we go:

(➡ from left to right)

A A A A	A A A A	A A A A	A A A A
1 2 3 4	1 2 3 4	1 2 3 4	1 2 3 4
D D D D	D D D D	D D D D	D D D D
1 2 3 4	1 2 3 4	1 2 3 4	1 2 3 4
G G G G	G G G G	G G G G	G G G G
1 2 3 4	1 2 3 4	1 2 3 4	1 2 3 4

So far, you always counted 1 - 2 - 3 - 4 , 1 - 2 - 3 - 4 and so forth. The "pro's" do basically the same thing, but in a slightly different way. They count:

1 - 2 - 3 - 4   **2** - 2 - 3 - 4   **3** - 2 - 3 - 4   **4** - 2 - 3 - 4

Notice something? Sure: The first figure in a row of four indicates the number of each measure (another word for bar). If the harmony changes you start counting again.
I'll explain what a bar (measure) is on the next page.

Now you are ready to play along to the Blues with me. Count out loud and play:

TAKE 3

A A A A	A A A A	A A A A	A A A A
1 2 3 4	**2** 2 3 4	**3** 2 3 4	**4** 2 3 4
D D D D	D D D D	A A A A	A A A A
1 2 3 4	**2** 2 3 4	**1** 2 3 4	**2** 2 3 4
E E E E	D D D D	A A A A	A A A A
1 2 3 4	**1** 2 3 4	**1** 2 3 4	**2** 2 3 4

21

In standard notation what you've just played looks like this:

O.K. You probably won't believe it, but this was an authentic Blues in the key of A.
Note: Normally a Blues consists of 12 bars, like the example above.

In the next example, you will accompany me by repeating the note sequence of Take 3, while I am playing a melody over your notes.

TAKE 4

The Basics

In order to be able to communicate musically, we use two separate notation systems in this book. You've already been introduced to one of them. It's called standard notation.
But let's start with the easier one: Tabulature (TAB) notation. The lines in the TAB basically indicate the four strings of the bass.

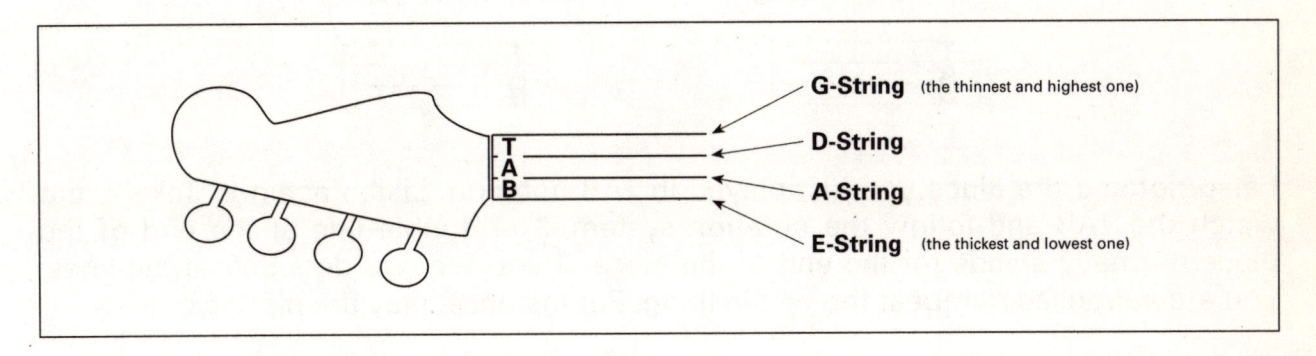

G-String (the thinnest and highest one)
D-String
A-String
E-String (the thickest and lowest one)

Those TAB-lines are divided up into measures:

bar 1   bar 2

bar 3   bar 4

and so forth

In the following example, each bar consists of four beats of equal length:

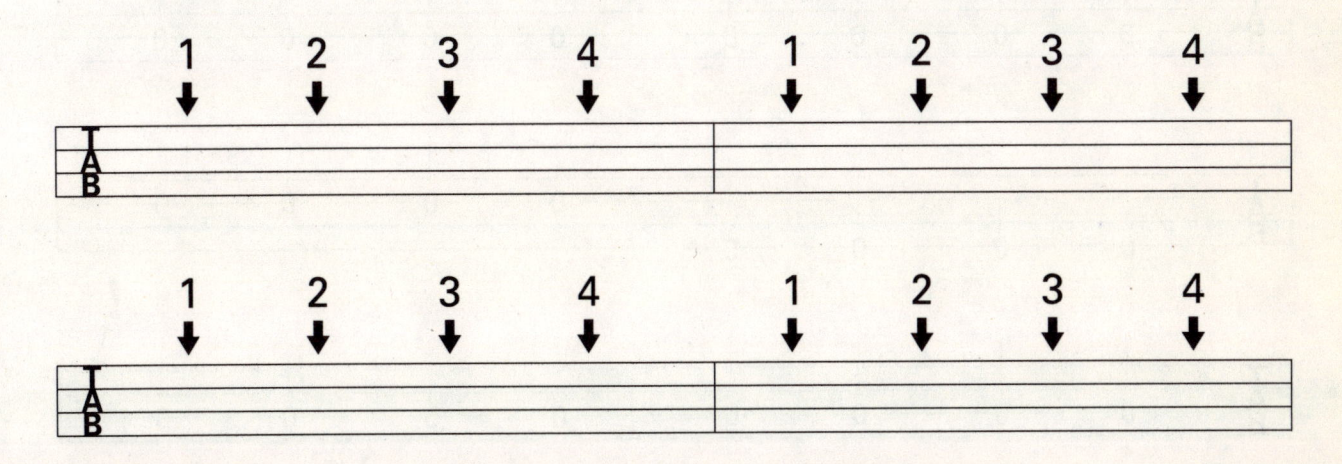

1   2   3   4   1   2   3   4

1   2   3   4   1   2   3   4

An "0" on a line means: play the indicated string without fretting a note (open string).

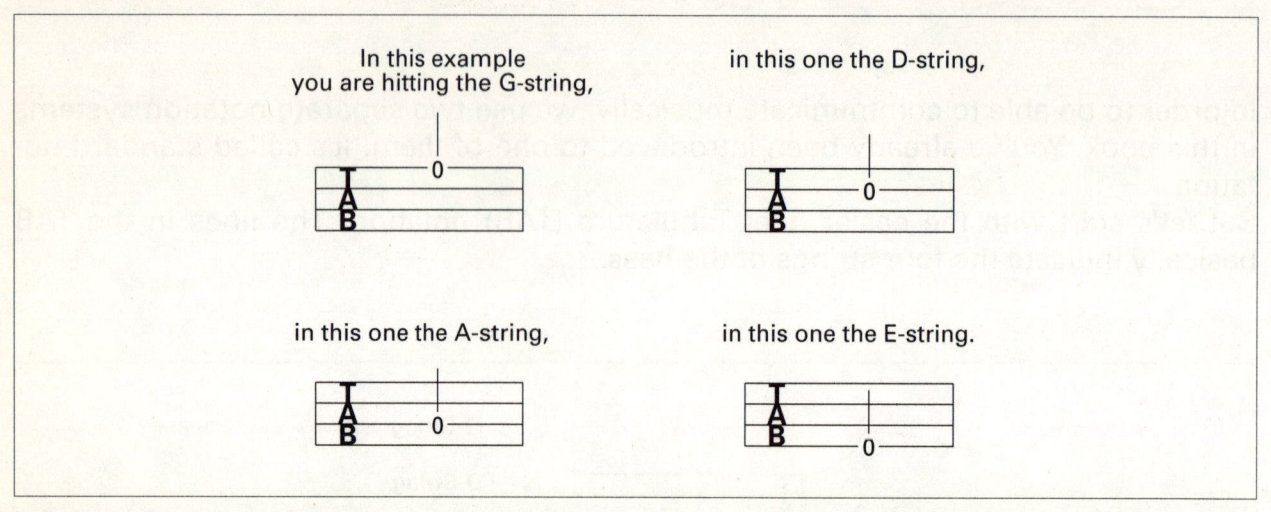

In this example you are hitting the G-string,

in this one the D-string,

in this one the A-string,

in this one the E-string.

I also notated the Blues you just played in TAB notation. Listen again to Take 2, but watch the TAB and follow the notation system. The double line at the end of the piece normally stands for the end of the piece. If you see two dots before the lines, you are supposed to repeat the whole thing. For instance, play the piece twice.

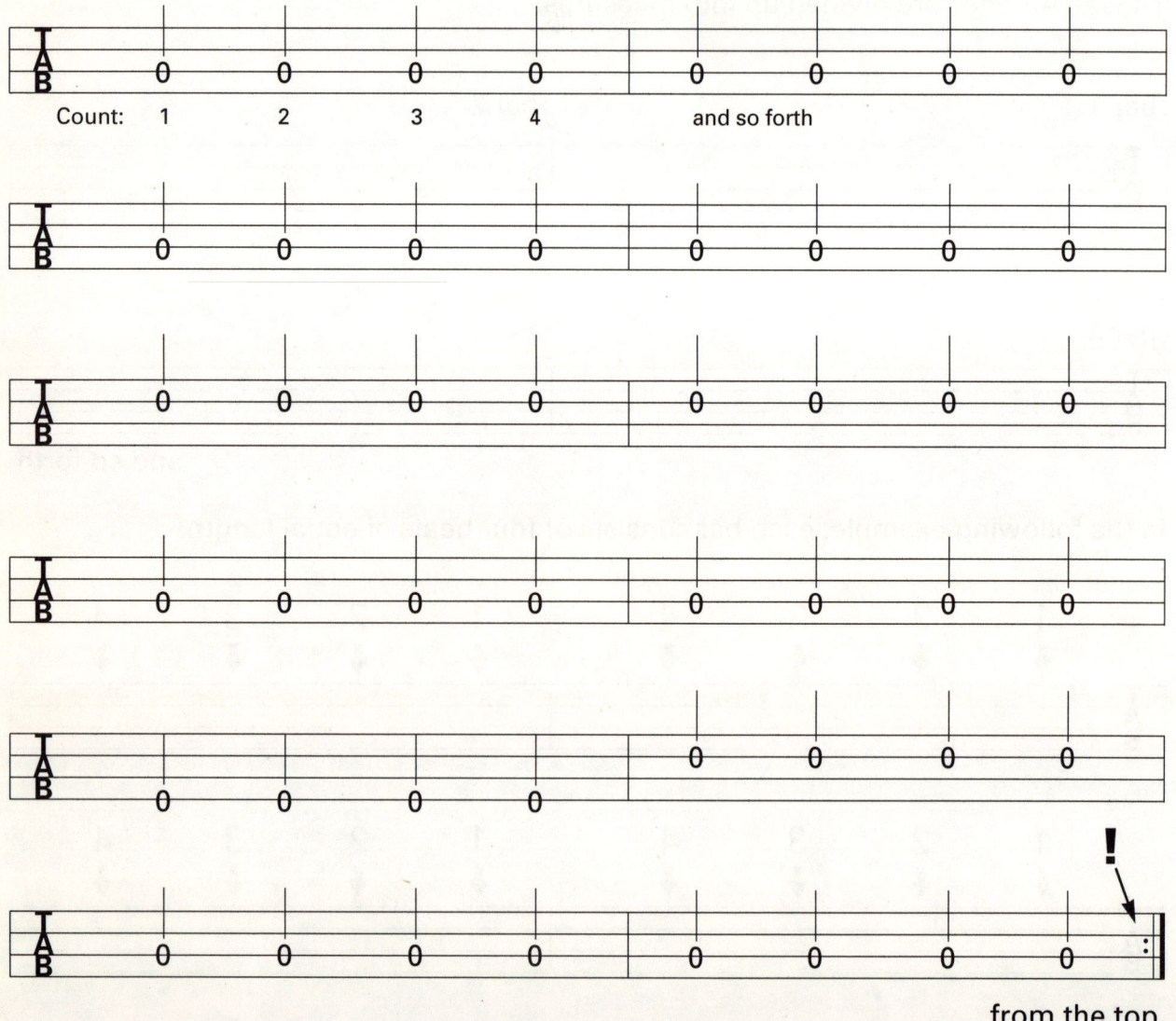

Count: 1 2 3 4   and so forth

from the top

24

The notes you were playing so far were "open strings". You know from the description of bass guitars that your instrument's fretboard is divided up into frets. And this is what we'll focus on:

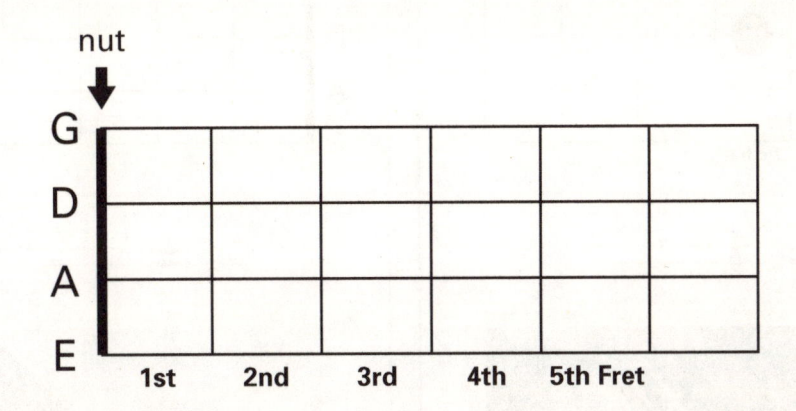

```
         nut
          ↓
    G ┌───┬───┬───┬───┬───┐
    D ├───┼───┼───┼───┼───┤
    A ├───┼───┼───┼───┼───┤
    E └───┴───┴───┴───┴───┘
       1st  2nd  3rd  4th  5th Fret
```

If you press down the G-string with the index finger of your left hand on the 2nd fret,

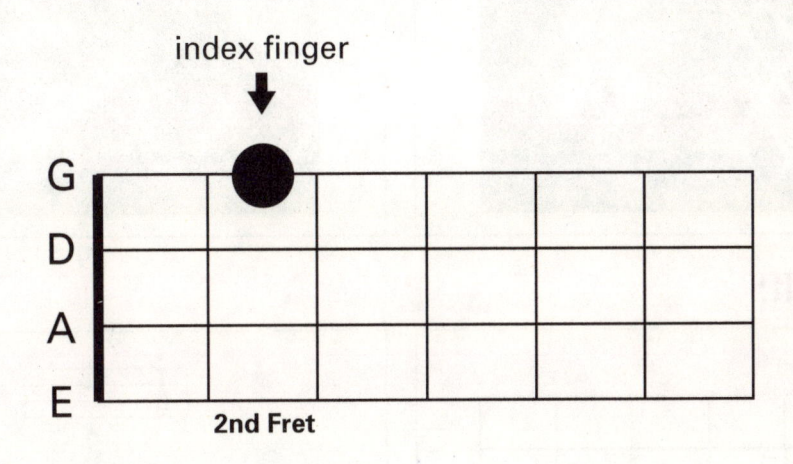

```
          index finger
               ↓
               ●
    G ┌───┬───┬───┬───┬───┐
    D ├───┼───┼───┼───┼───┤
    A ├───┼───┼───┼───┼───┤
    E └───┴───┴───┴───┴───┘
         2nd Fret
```

it looks like this in TAB notation:

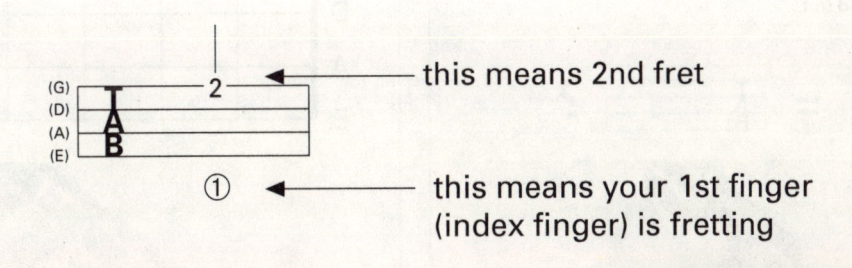

```
(G) ─────2─────   ← this means 2nd fret
(D) ──T──────
(A) ──A──────
(E) ──B──────
         ①       ← this means your 1st finger
                   (index finger) is fretting
```

The fingers are named as follows:

① = index finger
② = middle finger
③ = ring finger
④ = little finger

25

Two further examples:

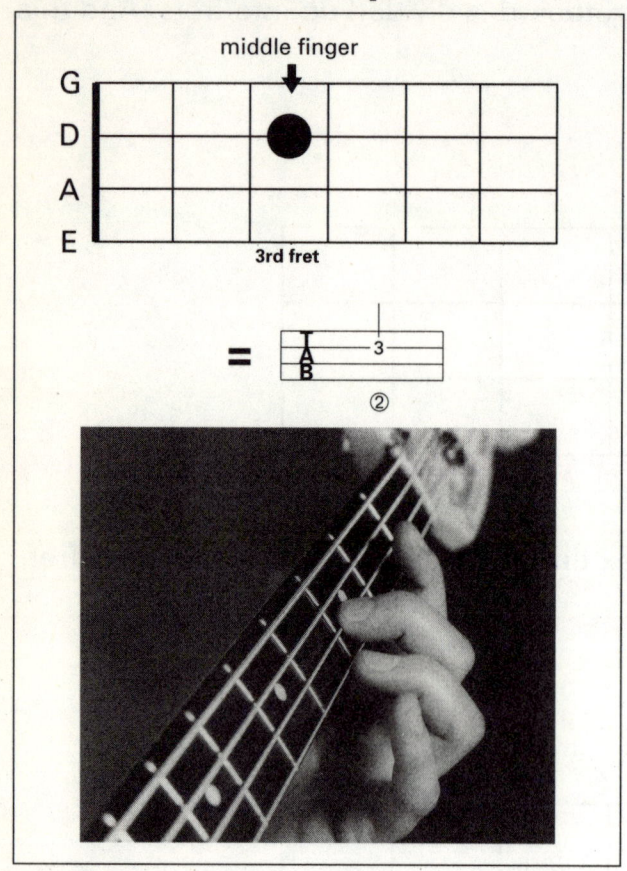

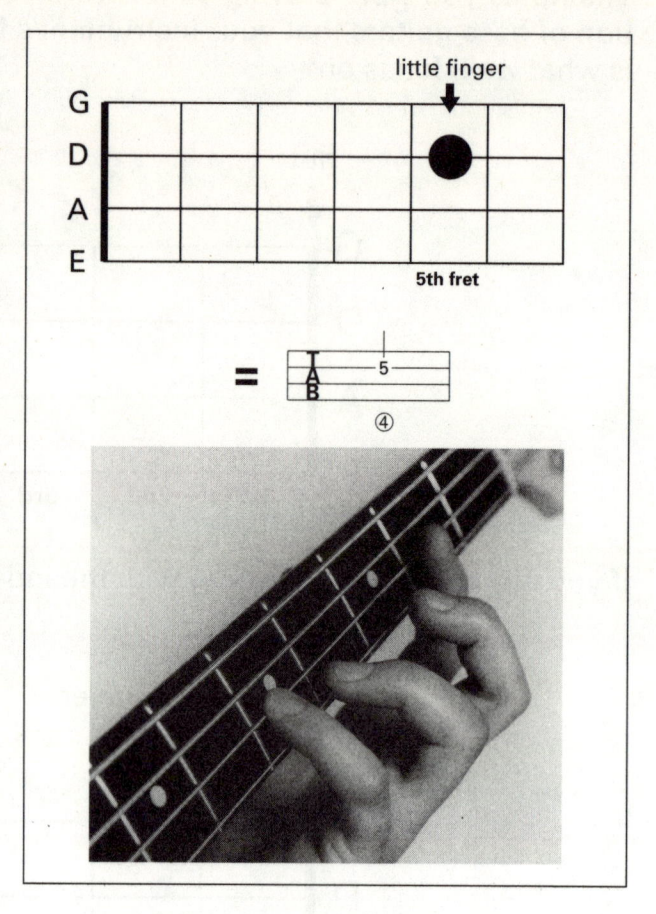

middle finger ↓
G D A E — 3rd fret

= TAB 3 ②

little finger ↓
G D A E — 5th fret

= TAB 5 ④

Test yourself:

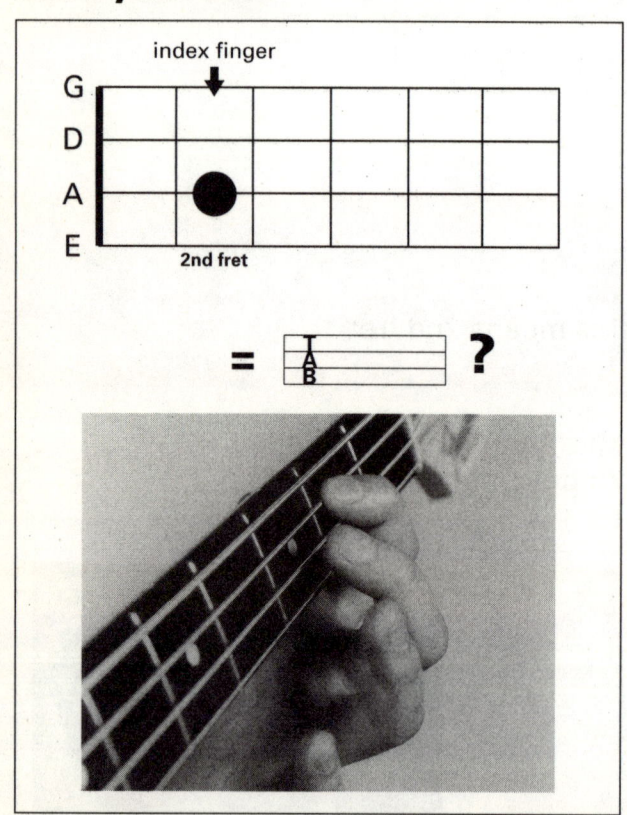

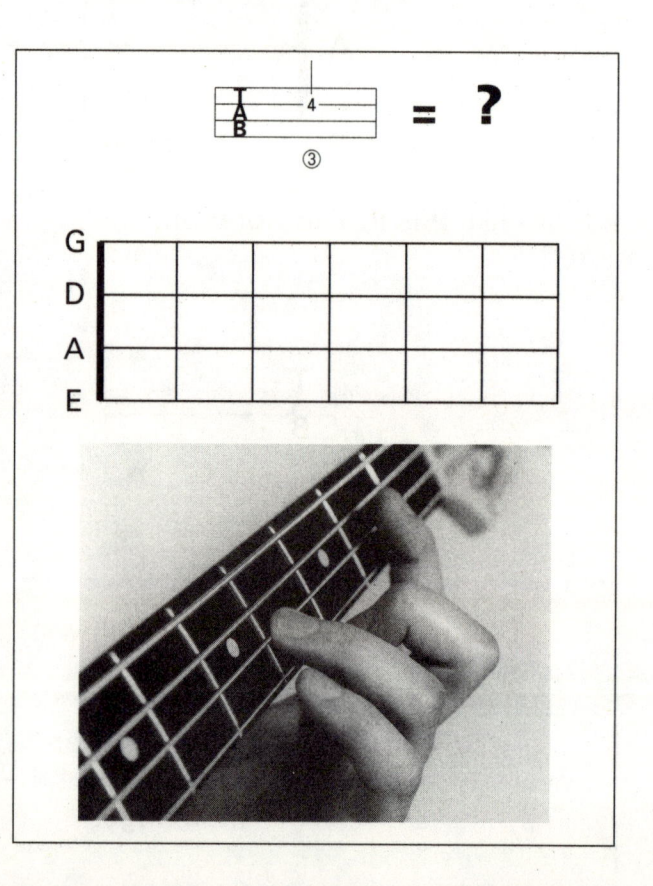

index finger ↓
G D A E — 2nd fret

= TAB ?

TAB 4 ③ = ?

G D A E

Pass the test? Cool: Your prize is the next bass line. Listen to Take 5 and play along.

26

TAKE 5

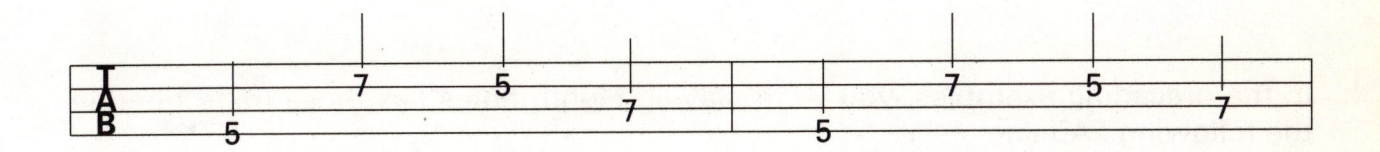

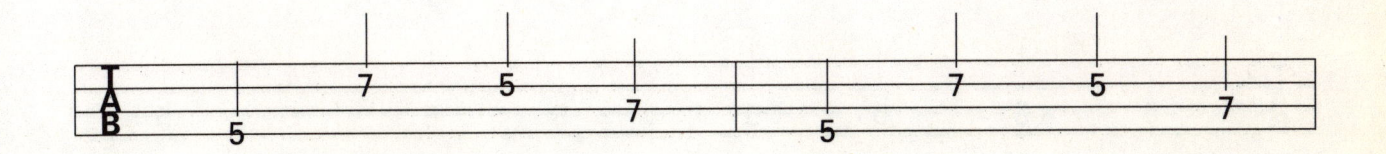

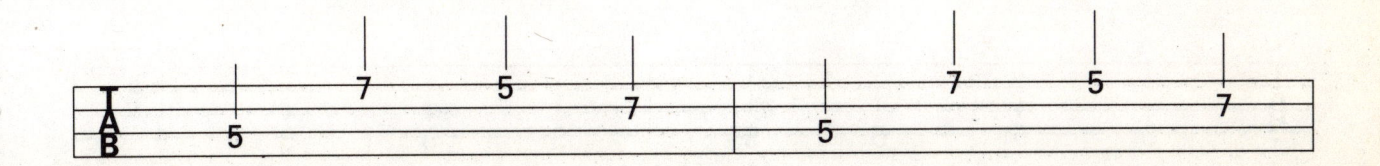

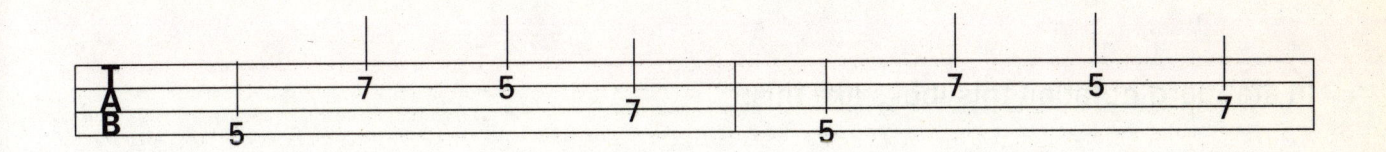

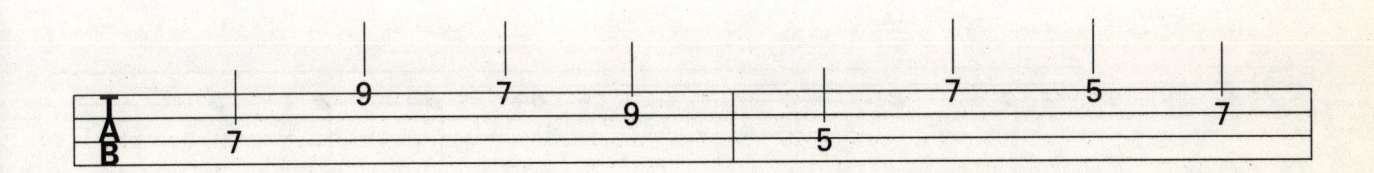

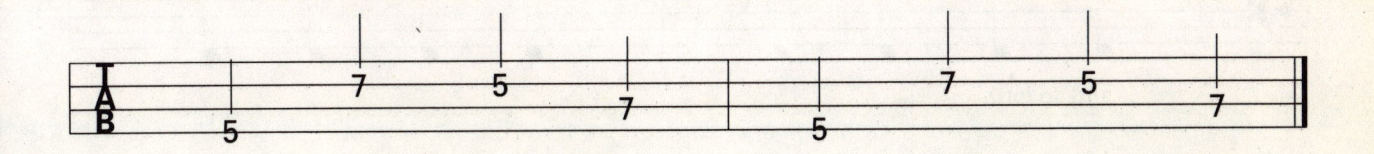

Let's go, but "in time"

In the preceding examples, you were playing eighth notes like those transcribed in the following TAB-line:

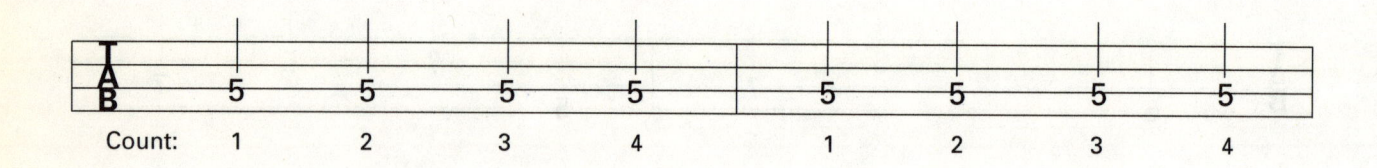

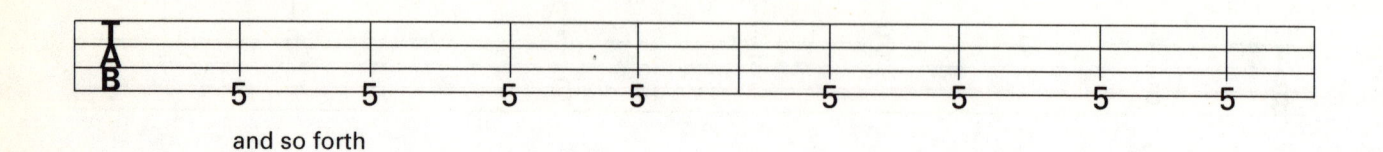

and so forth

In standard notation this looks like this:

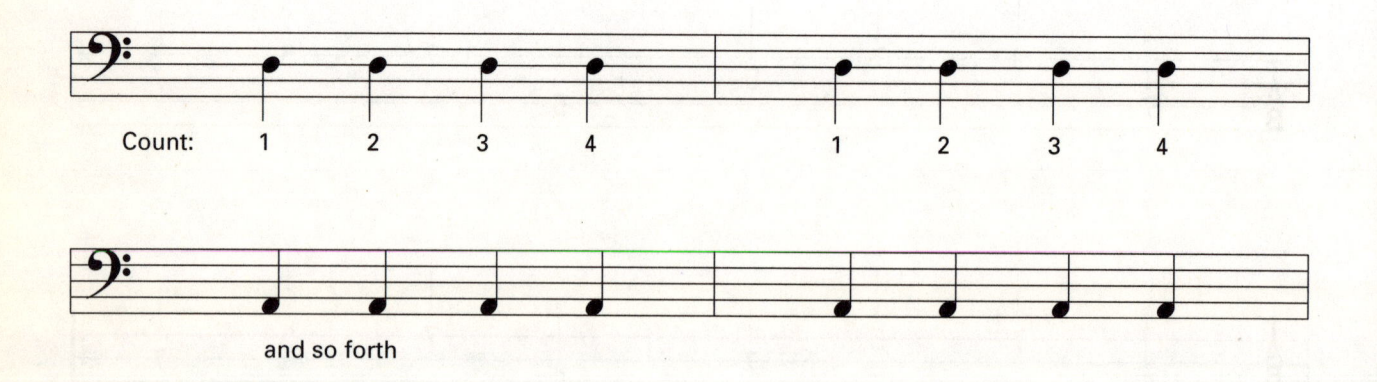

and so forth

Half notes are held twice as long as quarter notes and look like this:

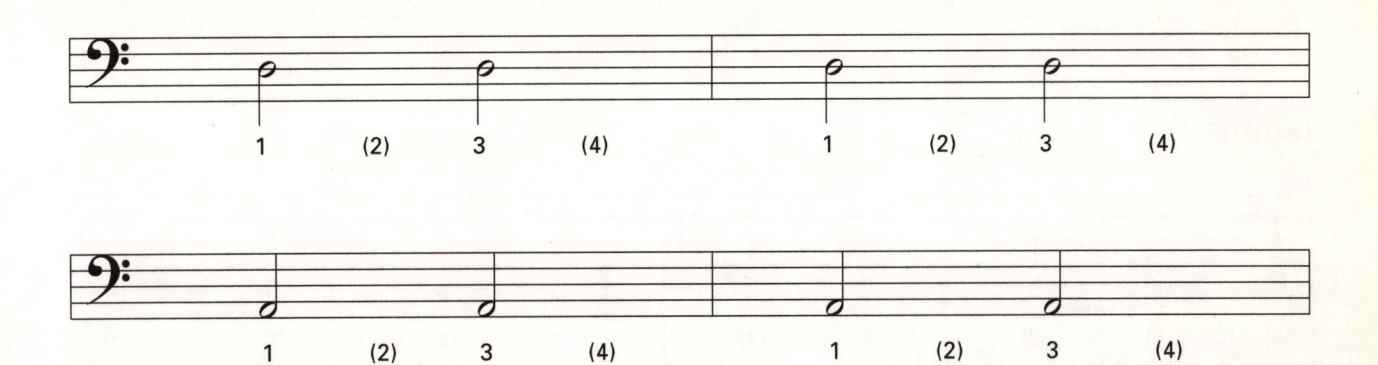

```
1   (2)   3   (4)    1   (2)   3   (4)

1   (2)   3   (4)    1   (2)   3   (4)
```

And here are half notes in TAB notation:

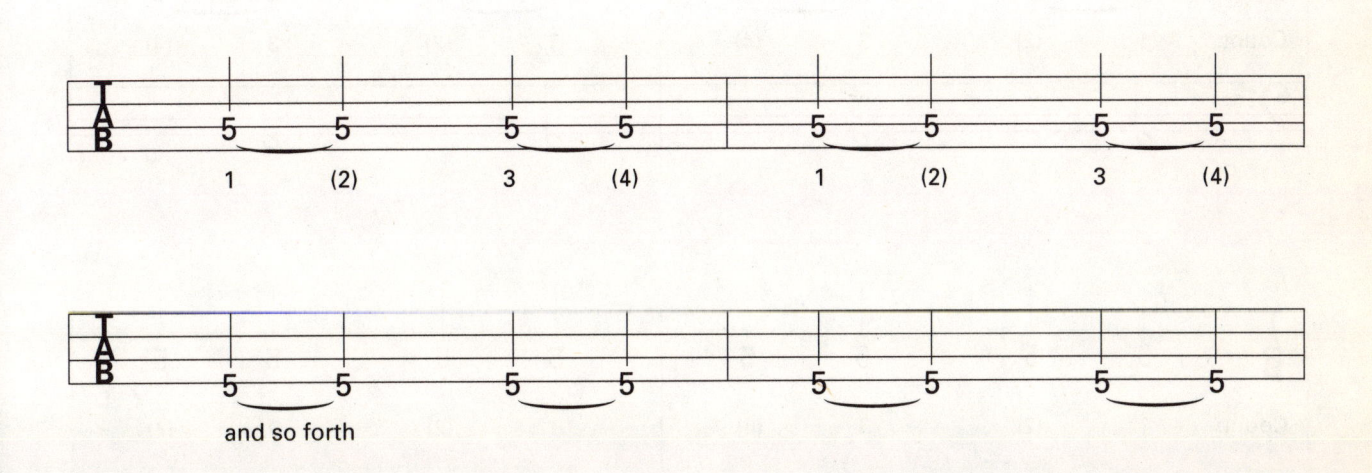

```
5----5    5----5    5----5    5----5
1   (2)   3   (4)   1   (2)   3   (4)

5----5    5----5    5----5    5----5
and so forth
```

Just imagine the note values in "brackets" (do not play them), i.e., you only play the first and third note (but hold it twice as long), so you count **1** - 2 - **3** - 4.
In order to show this in TAB notation, **the notes are tied**, making one note out of two notes.

Blues with Half Notes

(Key of A)

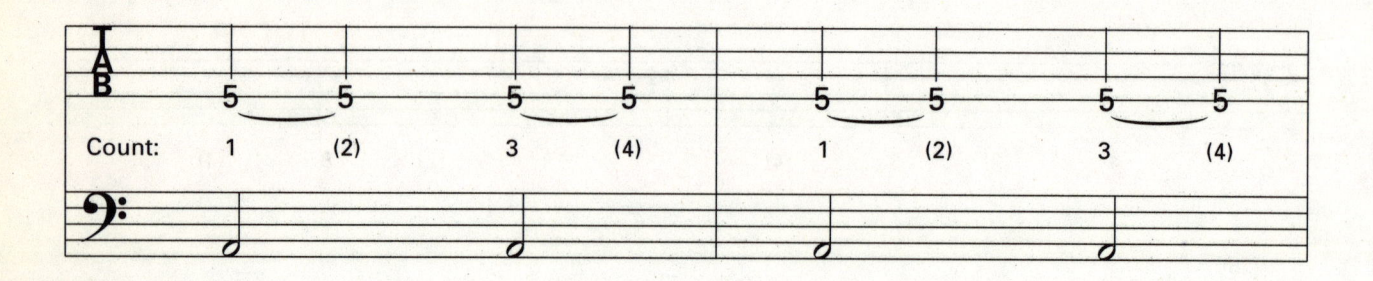

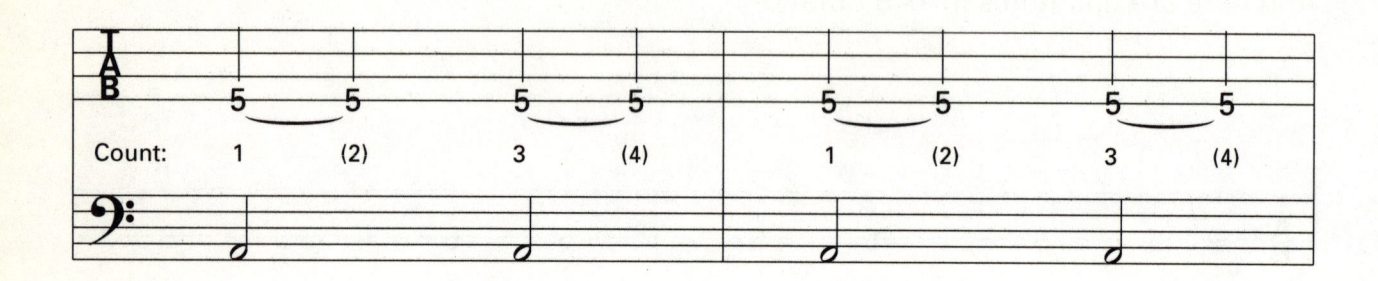

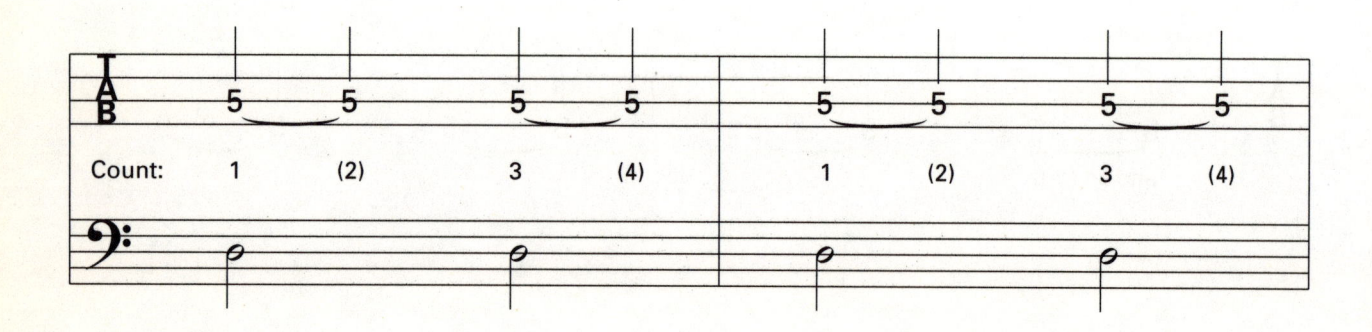

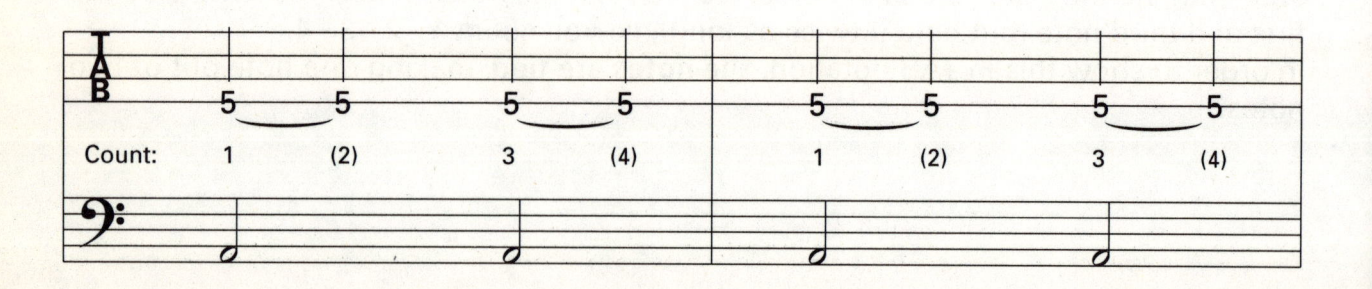

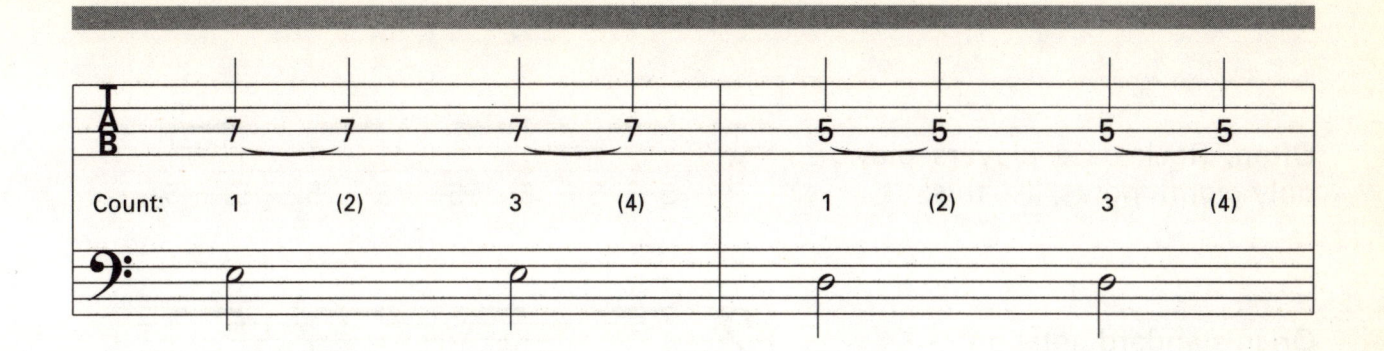

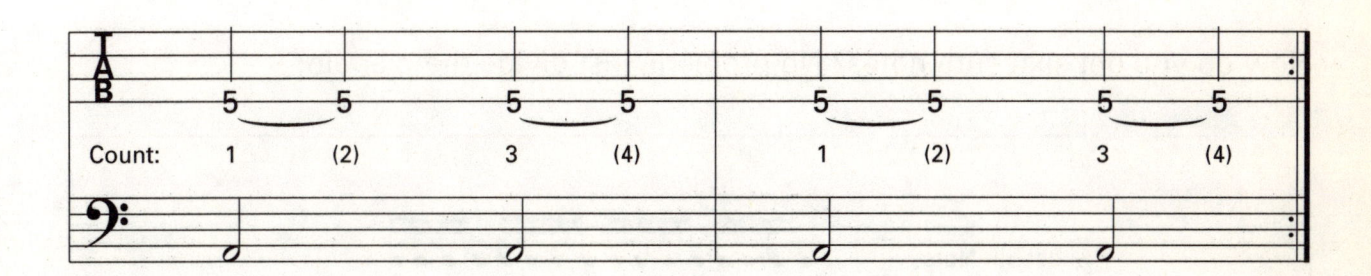

Before we continue, let's reinforce what we've just learned: One half note (𝅗𝅥) is twice as long as a quarter note (♩).

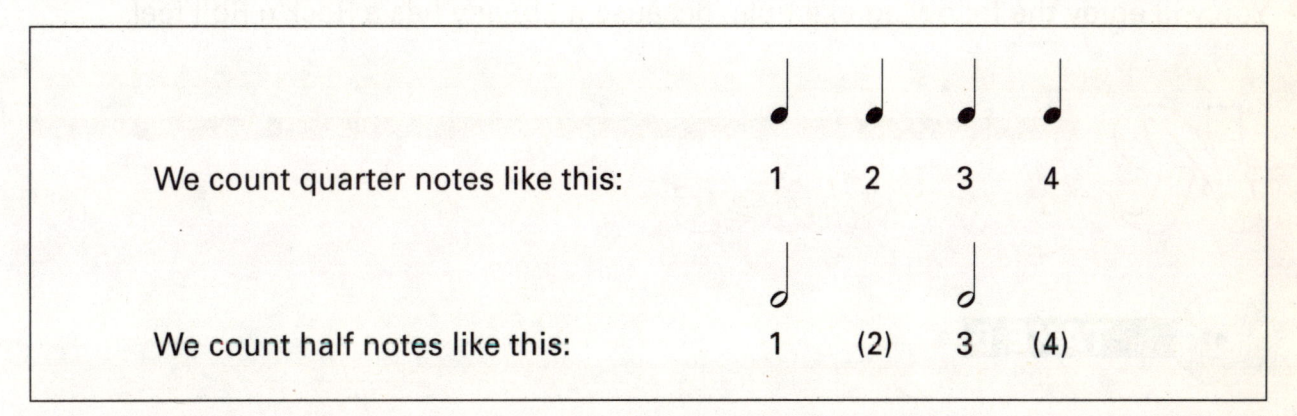

We count quarter notes like this: 1 2 3 4

We count half notes like this: 1 (2) 3 (4)

If we divide the quarter notes, we get eighth notes (watch how we count: 1 and 2 and 3 and...):

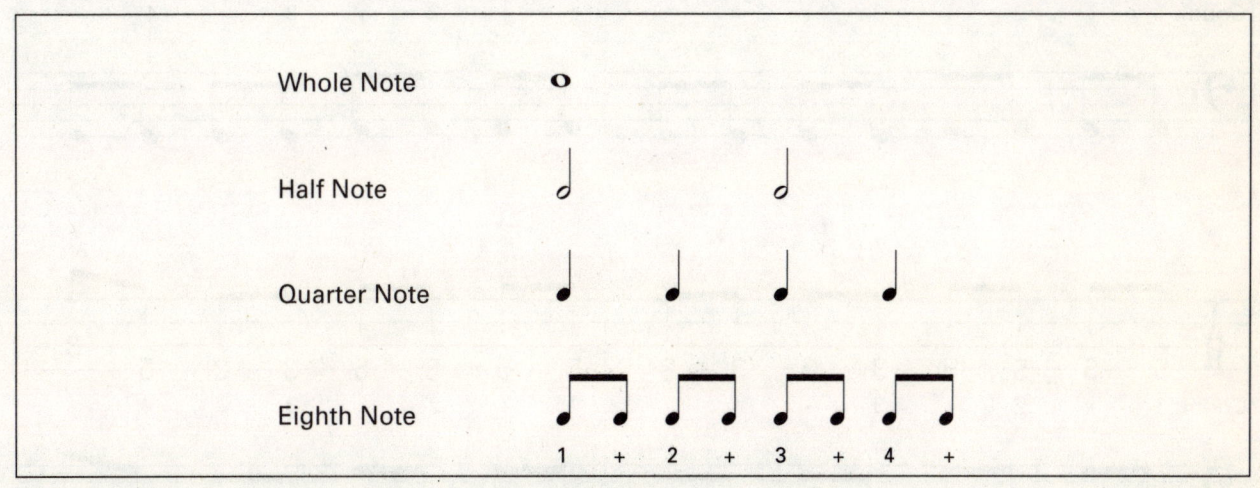

Whole Note
Half Note
Quarter Note
Eighth Note
1 + 2 + 3 + 4 +

Those notes form one measure (as explained on page 23).

Often, Rock bass players play only eighth notes, like this:

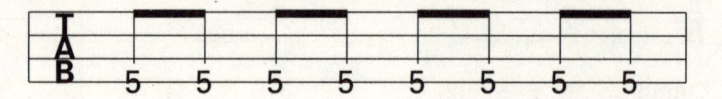

Or; in standard notation:

How do you get sixteenth notes? No problem, just divide them again:

Sixteenth Notes

You will enjoy the following example, because it already has a Rock'n'Roll feel.

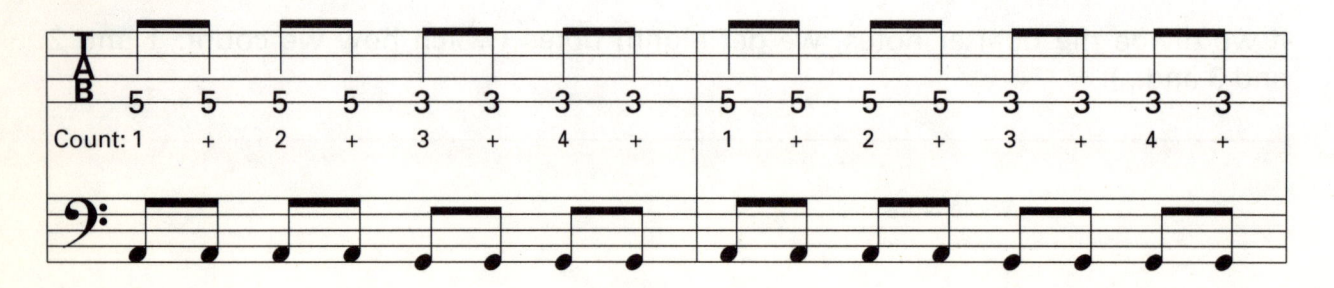

Rock Blues

TAKE 6

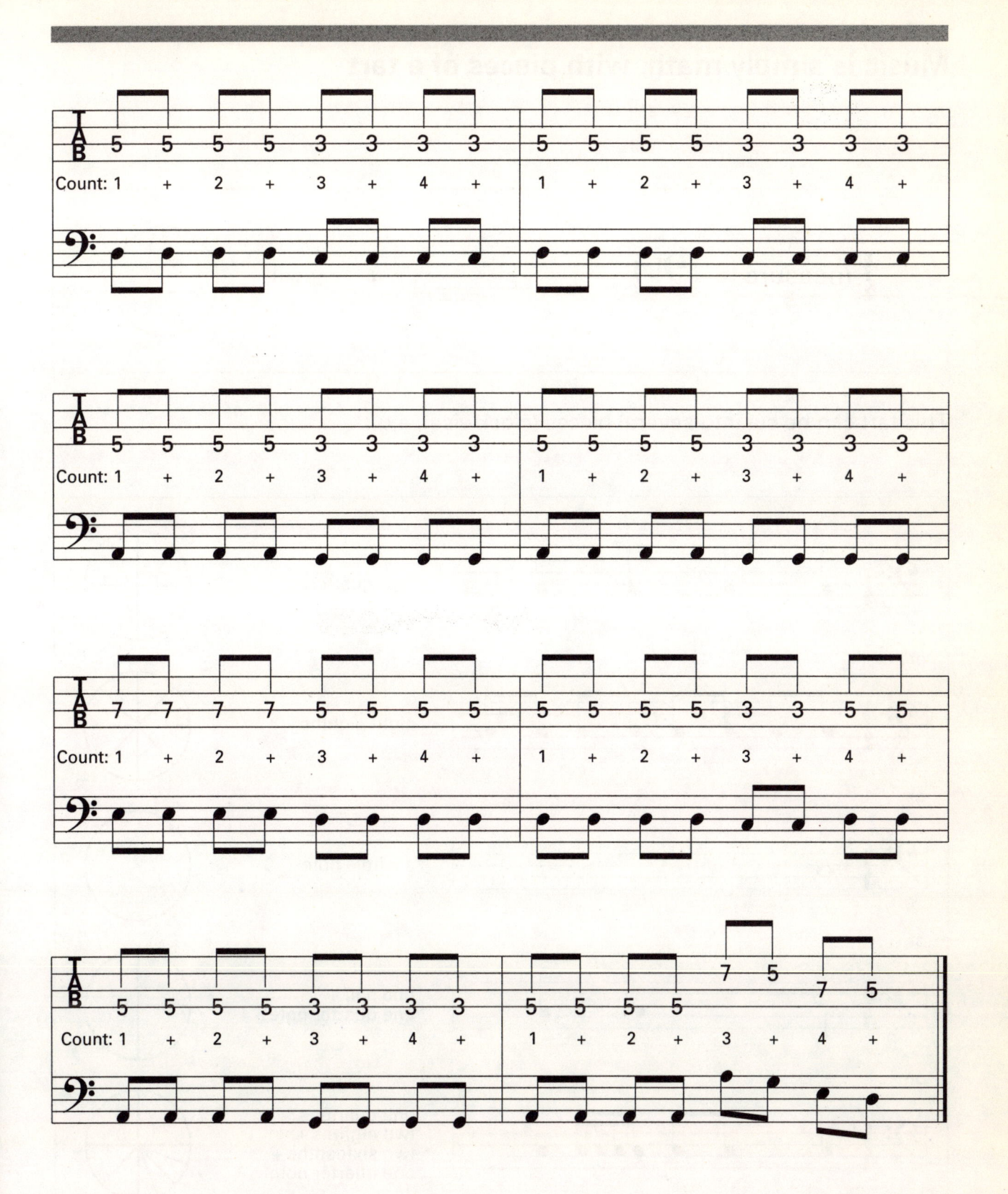

Make sure you always play without cramping your muscles. Keep your hand loose at all times.

Music is simply math, with pieces of a tart

4/4 measure = [bass clef 4/4 staff] = one tart ○

This tart can be cut into several pieces (clockwise), e.g.:

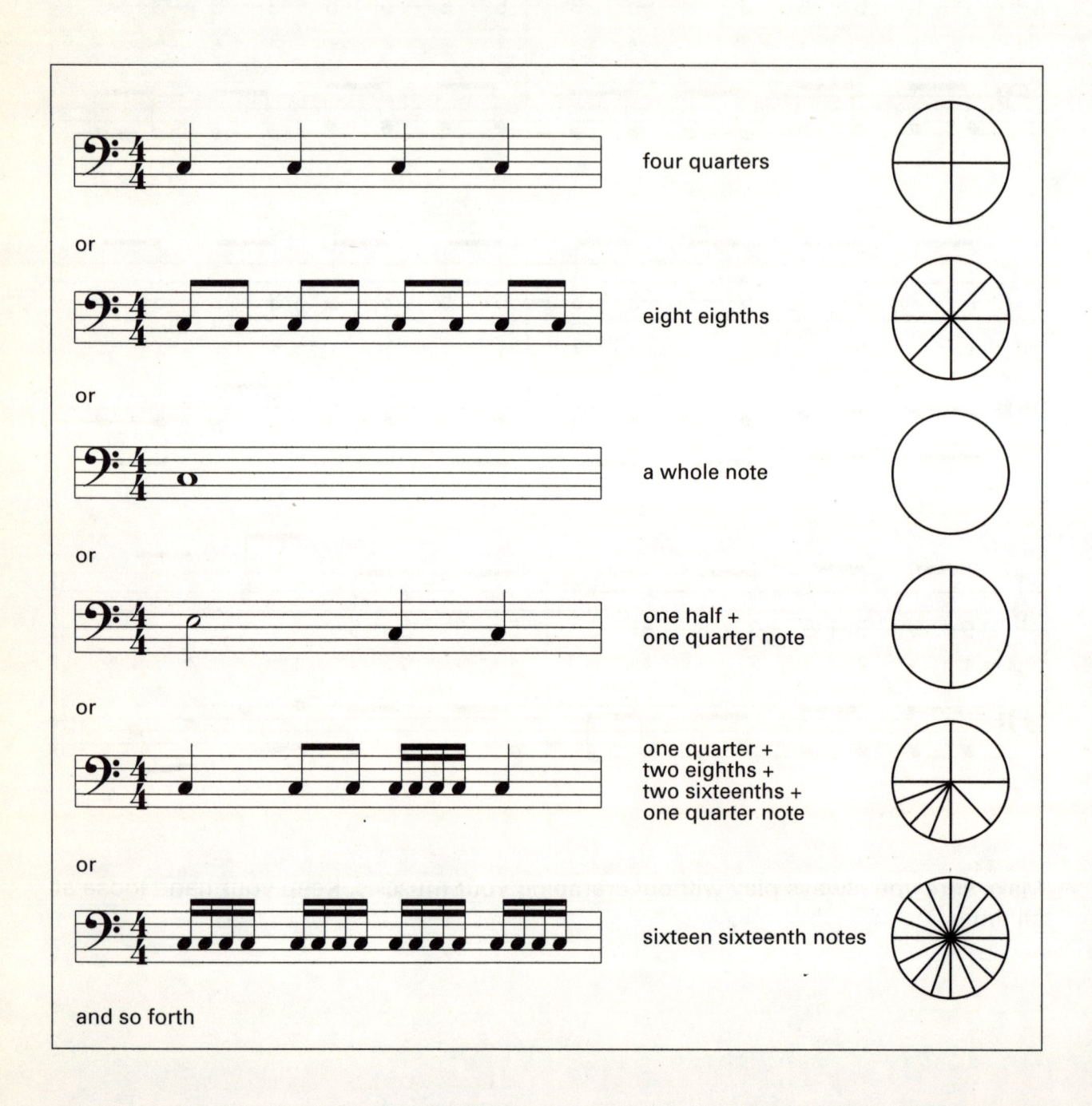

[bass clef 4/4: four quarter notes] — four quarters

or

[bass clef 4/4: eight eighth notes] — eight eighths

or

[bass clef 4/4: whole note] — a whole note

or

[bass clef 4/4: half note + two quarter notes] — one half + one quarter note

or

[bass clef 4/4: quarter + two eighths + two sixteenths + quarter] — one quarter + two eighths + two sixteenths + one quarter note

or

[bass clef 4/4: sixteen sixteenth notes] — sixteen sixteenth notes

and so forth

34

If the tart cannot be filled with notes, it has to be filled up with rests. For example:

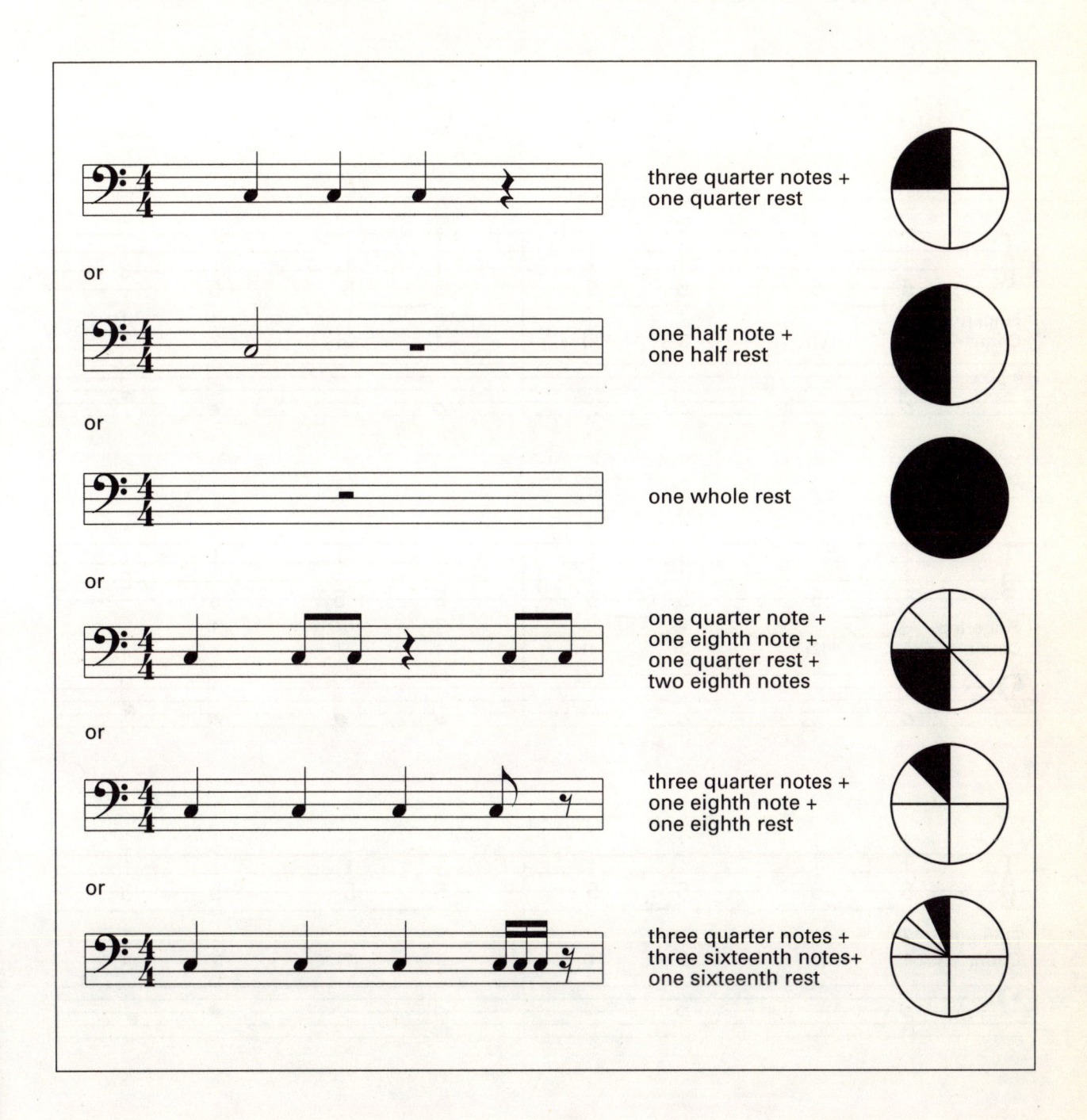

three quarter notes +
one quarter rest

or

one half note +
one half rest

or

one whole rest

or

one quarter note +
one eighth note +
one quarter rest +
two eighth notes

or

three quarter notes +
one eighth note +
one eighth rest

or

three quarter notes +
three sixteenth notes +
one sixteenth rest

So far, so good. Now let the bigger pieces take care of the bigger appetite.

Blues in A with Half Notes and Quarter Notes

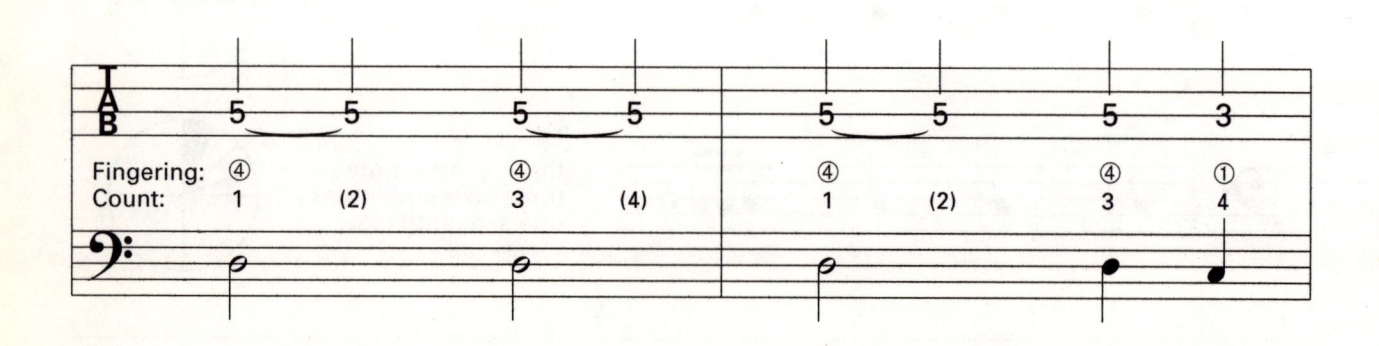

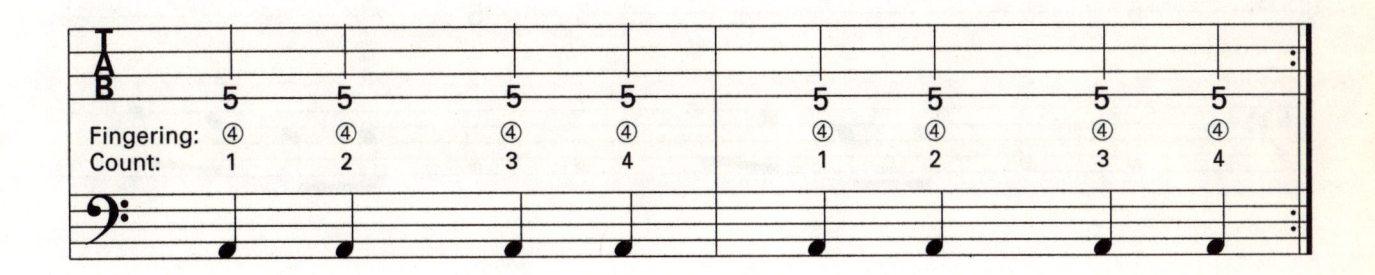

Practice the following bars separately:

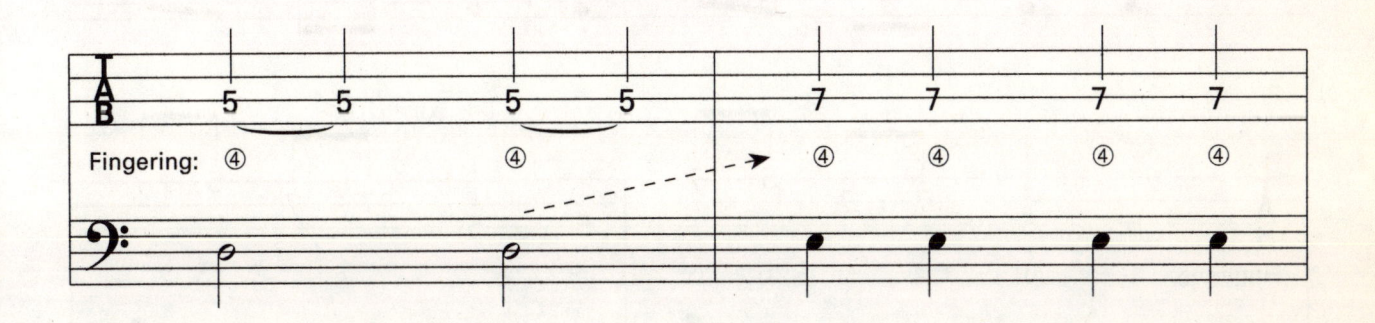

The constant fingering shows that you are only using your fourth finger. Thus, your hand is sliding up the neck two frets to play the notes.

Blues in A with Quarter and Eighth Notes

TAKE 7

Check if your playing is accurate (watch the fingering).
Practice bars separately and, once you know them, play along with the CD.

Blues in A with Eighth Notes

TAKE 8

Fingering: ② ② ④ ② ④ ② ④ ①   ② ② ④ ② ④ ② ④ ①

Fingering: ② ② ④ ② ④ ② ④ ①   and so forth

The fingering remains the same throughout the whole exercise. You only change the position of your right hand. This bass lick requires some flexibility from your fingers.
Make sure that you are fretting the notes properly. Pictured here is the correct position for your left hand.

Beware: Accidentals!

♯ ((e.g. G-sharp) = a note raised by one half tone
♭ (e.g. G-flat) = a note lowered by one half tone

Keep in mind!

Accidentals within a measure are only valid for the bar they are written in. They can be cancelled by this sign: ♮

Accidentals at the beginning of a piece indicate the key in which it is written. They are valid until a new key is indicated or cancelled by a ♮ sign. The ♮ sign then only "lasts" throughout the measure or the next ♯ oder ♭.

41

Blues-Solo in A

Start the CD and play along to the following melody:

TAKE 9 (In the background you'll hear the accompaniment of Take 8.)

Fingering: ④ ② ① ② ④
Count: 1 (2) 3 4 + 1 + 2 + 3 + 4 +

42

Fast Rock

Try to figure out the best fingering for yourself.

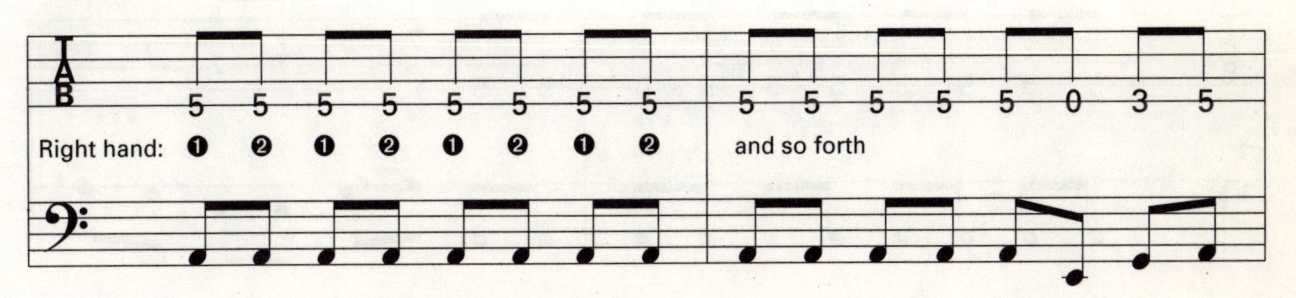

TAKE 10

43

This is a typical, powerful Rock pattern, due to it's characteristic eighth notes. The big deal is: playing precisely. As an exercise, you should try and play this line as fast as you can.

Remember: ♮ resolves ♯ and ♭.

Chapter 3

The "Stress-String"

The following exercises require concentration because every bar is different. Practice measure by measure and try not to get thrown out of the groove.

Very slowly!

It's a good sign if you haven't dislocated anything by now. Try to increase the tempo a little bit as you go.

Now let's continue with the following exercise, which you should repeat several times, constantly increasing the tempo:

Look out!
The second note of the exercise is a "G-sharp" which is being resolved by a ♮ to a regular "G".
The same thing happens in the sixth note of bar 2: a "D-sharp" becomes a "D", i.e., you play one half note lower.

Land Drill

For the next exercise, you don't need a bass guitar, just your hands for clapping. With this exercise, we will train your sense of rhythm, which is (any child knows that) the essence of Rock music.

Little hint:
It will be helpful to try and tap your foot on the downbeats (1, 2, 3, 4).

| Count: | 1 | (2) | (3) | (4) | 1 | (2) | (3) | (4) |

| Count: | 1 | (2) | (3) | (4) | 1 | (2) | (3) | (4) |

| Count: | 1 | (2) | 3 | (4) | 1 | (2) | 3 | (4) |

| Count: | 1 | (2) | 3 | (4) | 1 | (2) | 3 | (4) |

| Count: | 1 | 2 | 3 | 4 | 1 | 2 | 3 | 4 |

| Count: | 1 | 2 | 3 | 4 | 1 | 2 | 3 | 4 |

Count: 1   (2)   3   4   1   2   3   (4)

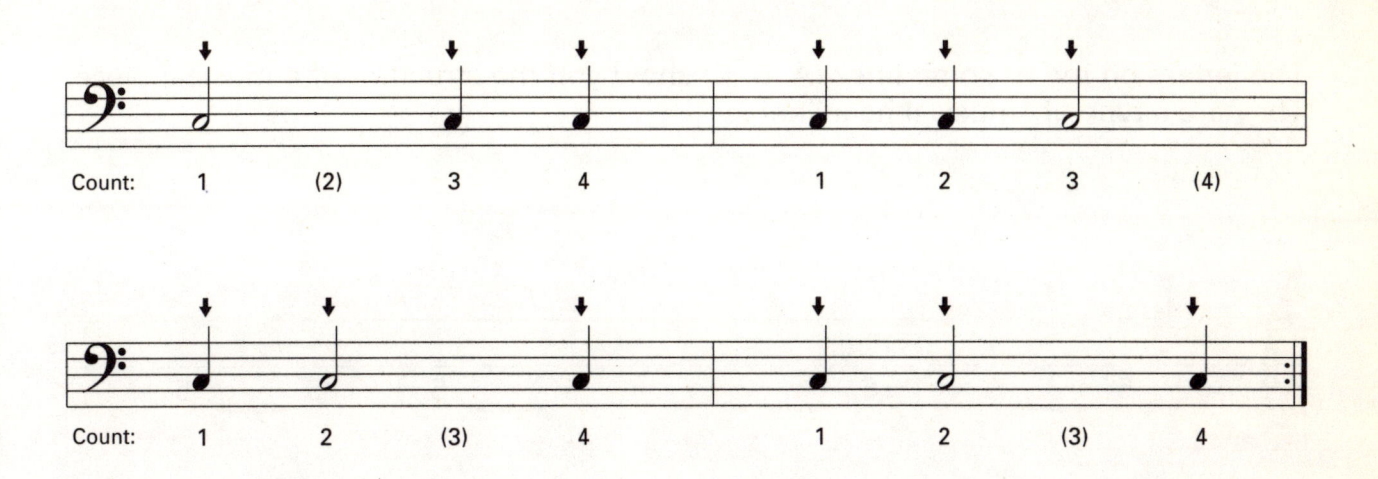

Count: 1   2   (3)   4   1   2   (3)   4

This clapping example shows you how to build up tension within a piece by doubling the notes per measure.
The Blues line on the following pages will illustrate this once again. Half notes become two quarter notes or four eighth notes.

Notate your own version of increased tension and practice it. Only use whole, half and quarter notes:

Blues

The letters on top of some lines (A, B, C) show you the structure of a musical piece. They are a type of "musical headline".

A

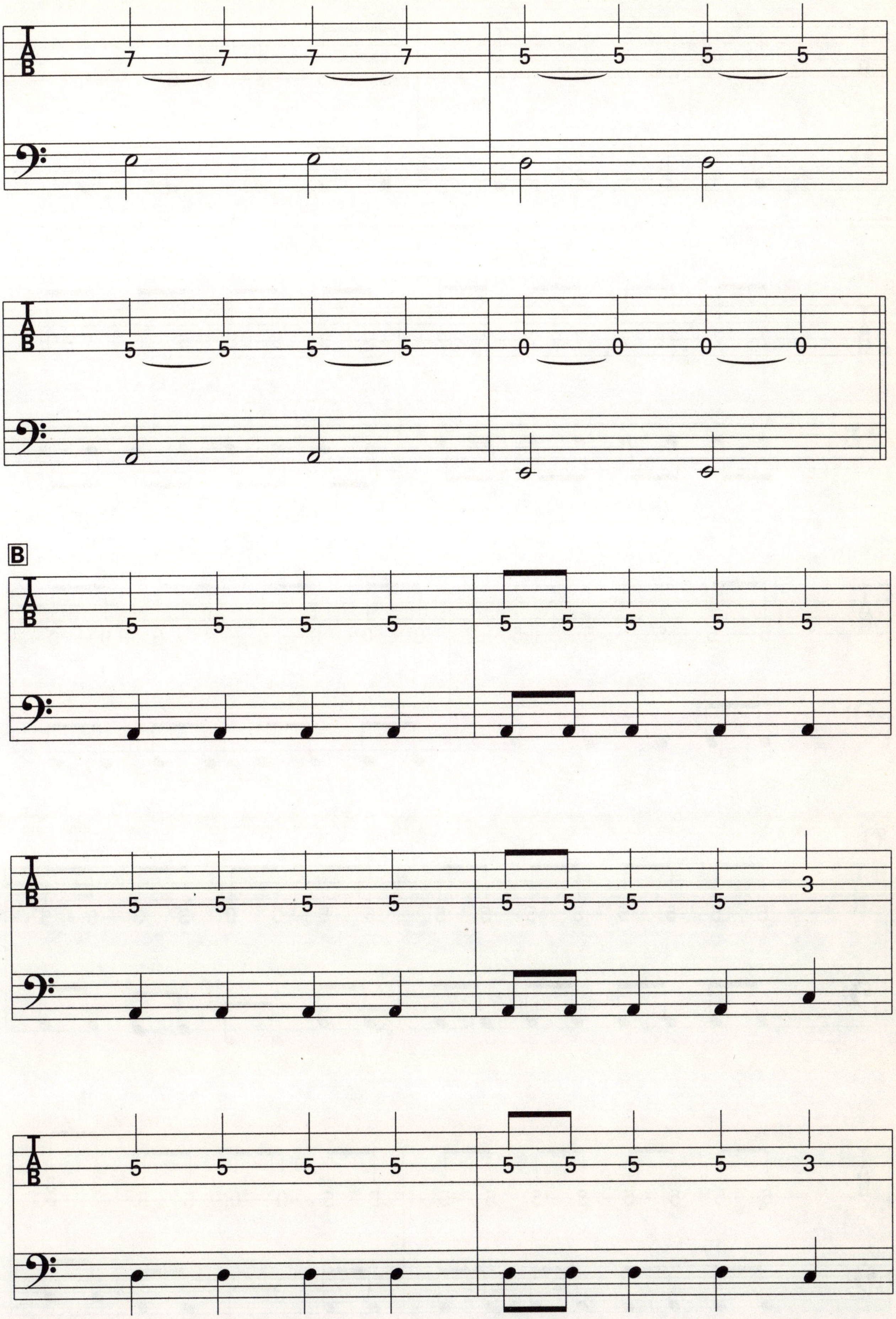

52

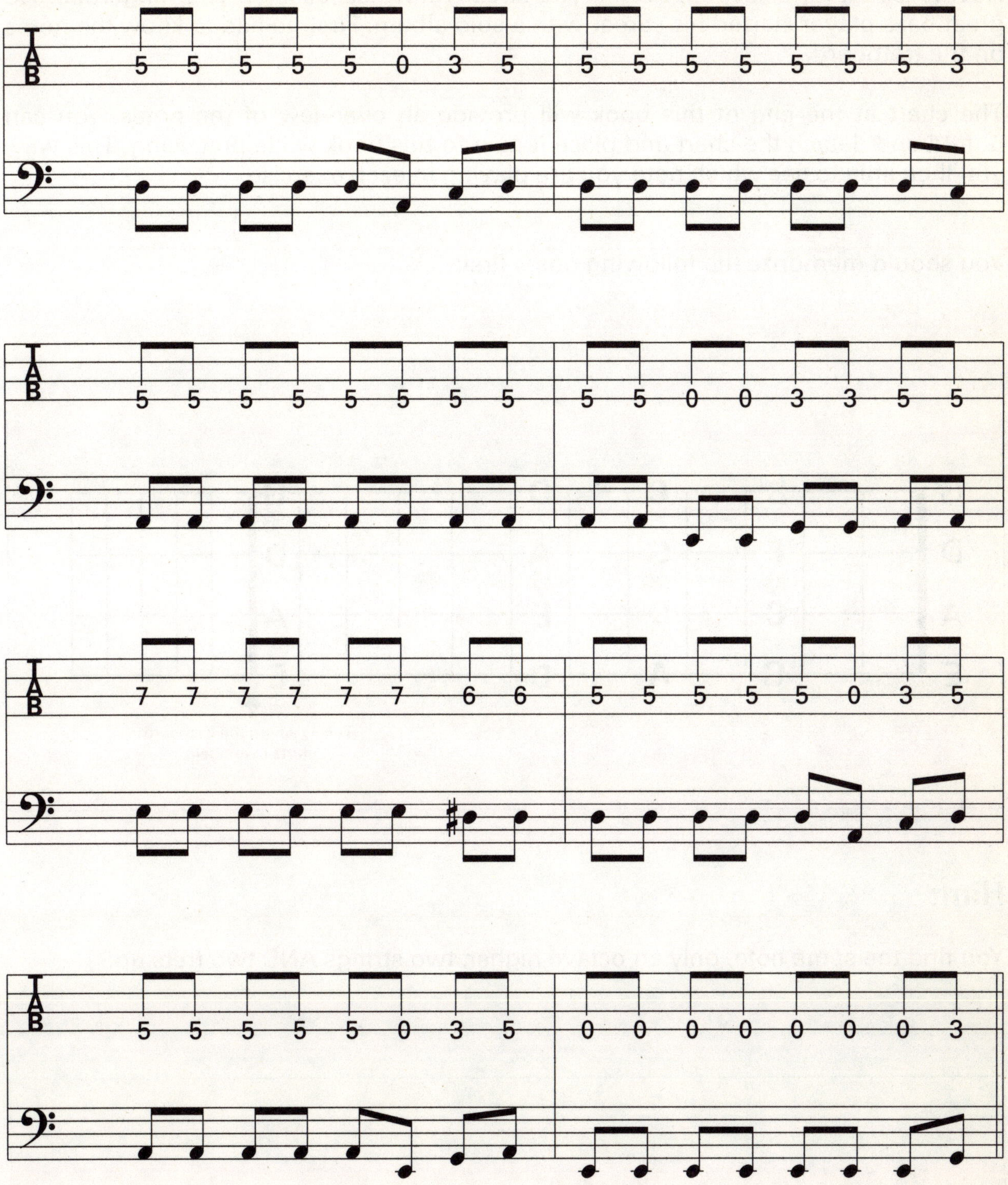

Now let's rest for a second, even if you already have calluses on your fingertips! No great bass player started his career with a solo album. First he had to know the notes on the fretboard.

The chart at the end of this book will provide an overview of the notes. You can unfold and detach the chart and place it next to this book while practicing. This way, you'll be able to see which note you are playing in each exercise.

You should memorize the following notes first:

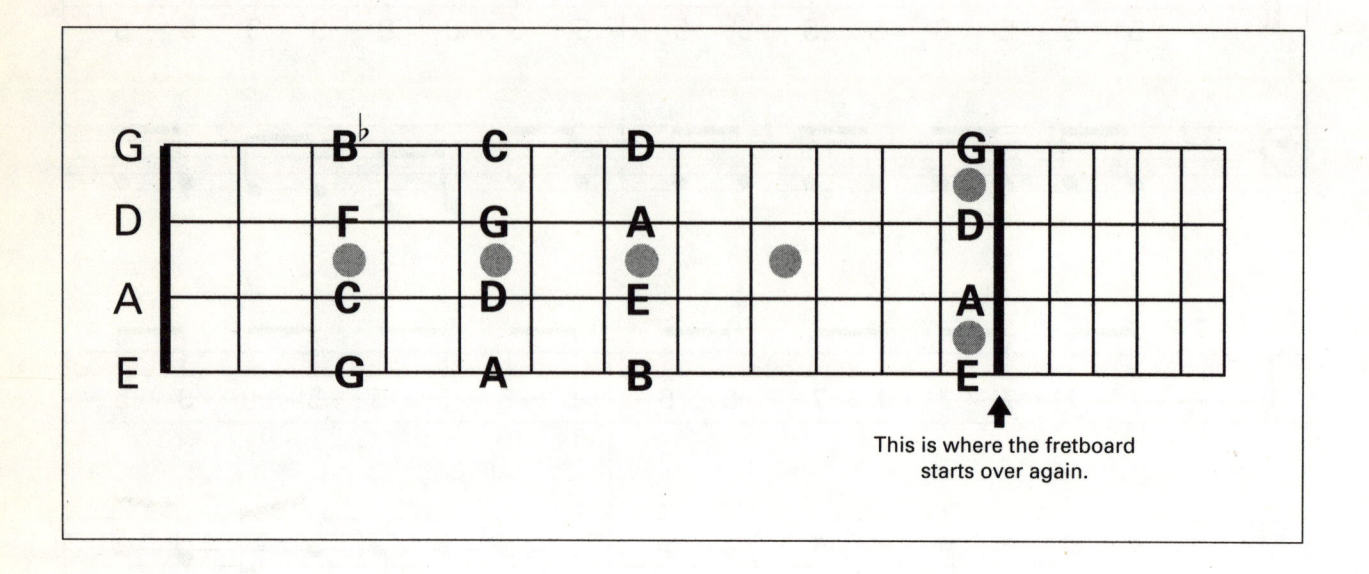

[fretboard diagram showing notes: G string: G, B♭, C, D, G; D string: D, F, G, A, D; A string: A, C, D, E, A; E string: E, G, A, B, E]

↑ This is where the fretboard starts over again.

Hint:

You find the same note, only an octave higher, two strings AND two frets up.

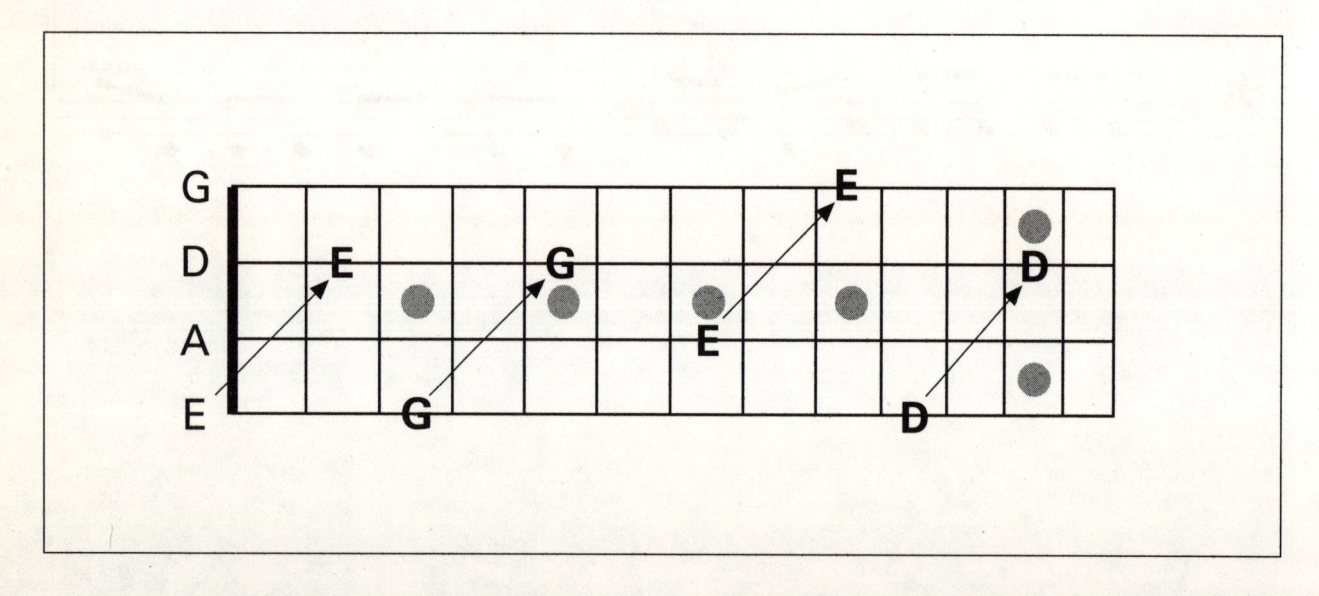

[fretboard diagram showing octave relationships with arrows: E→E, G→G, E→E, D→D]

The Key of C Major

To make a long story short, the key of C major consists of the following notes:

In standard notation

In TAB notation

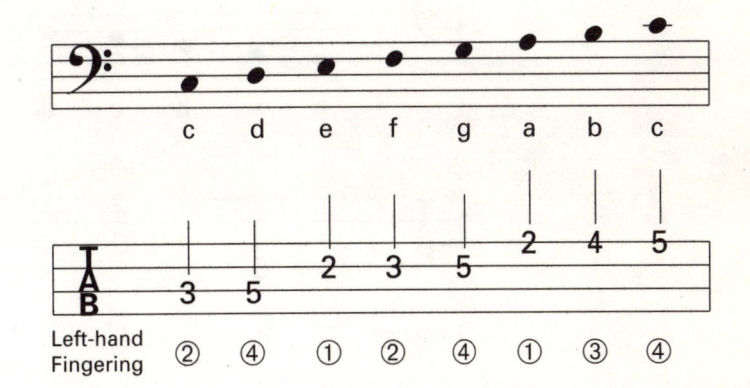

c d e f g a b c

Left-hand Fingering ② ④ ① ② ④ ① ③ ④

Note the hand position on the photo! Memorize the distance between the notes and the distance from fret to fret.
The good thing about basses (as well as guitars) is: Simply by shifting positions with your left hand, you can play in any other major key.

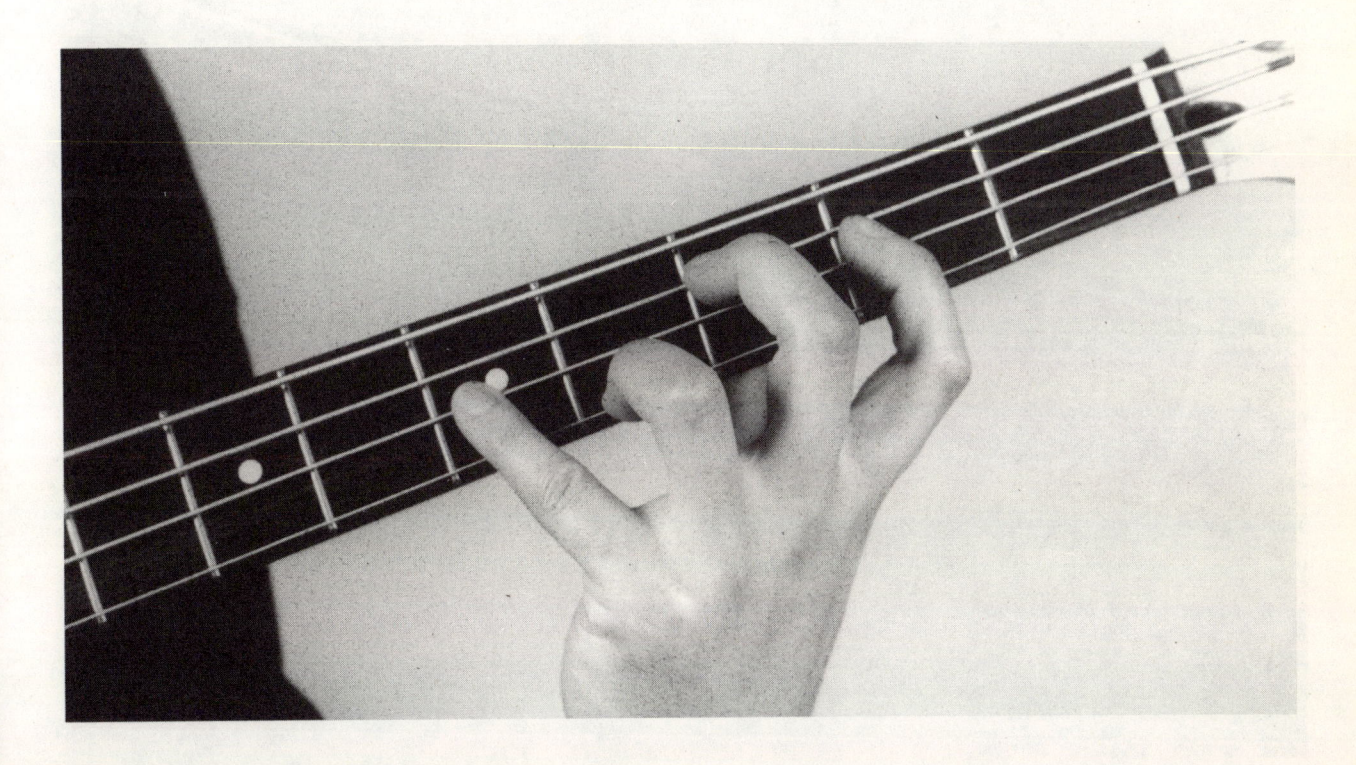

Your middle finger was placed on the "C". Now place it on the next lower string on the same fret (there's only one left anyway). Now you're in the key of G major. Do you remember the "distances" from the key of C major? - Now you're in "G".

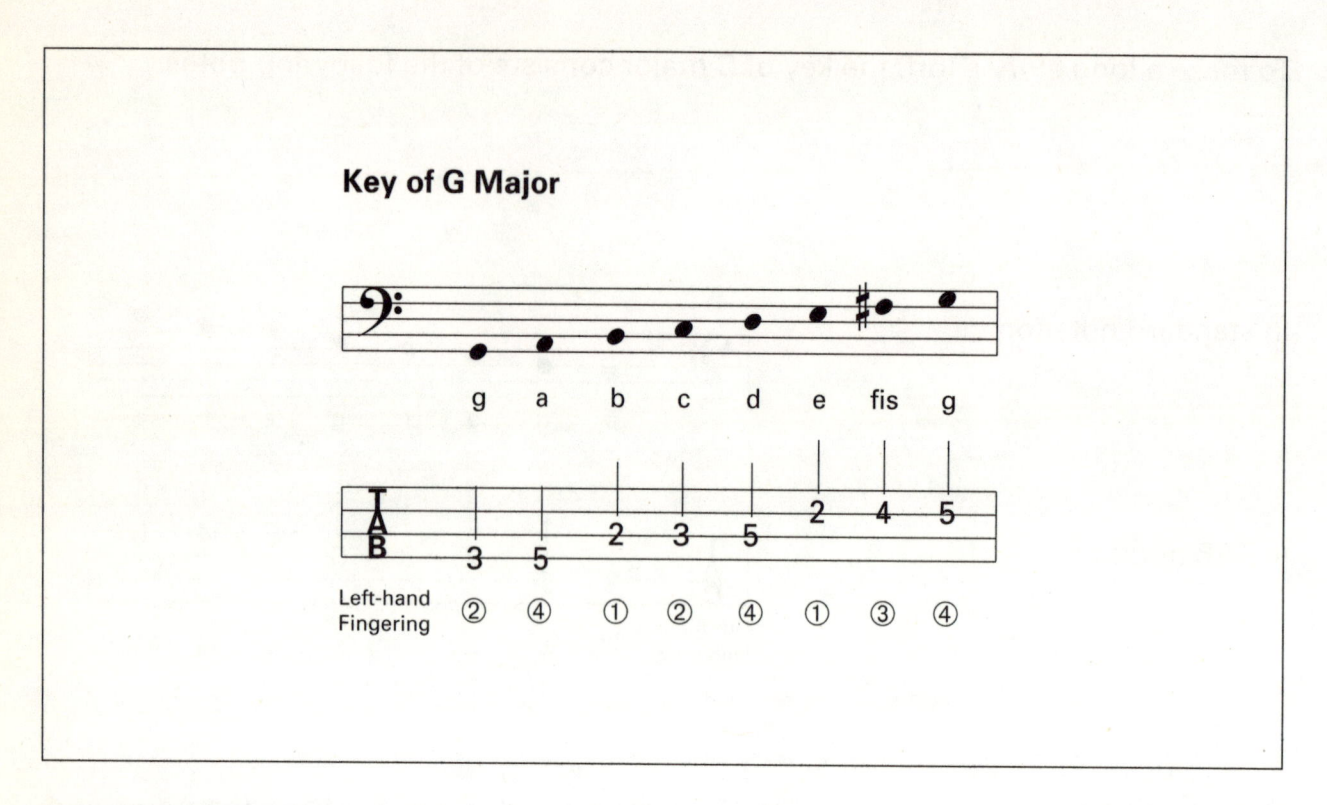

Key of G Major

Hand position:

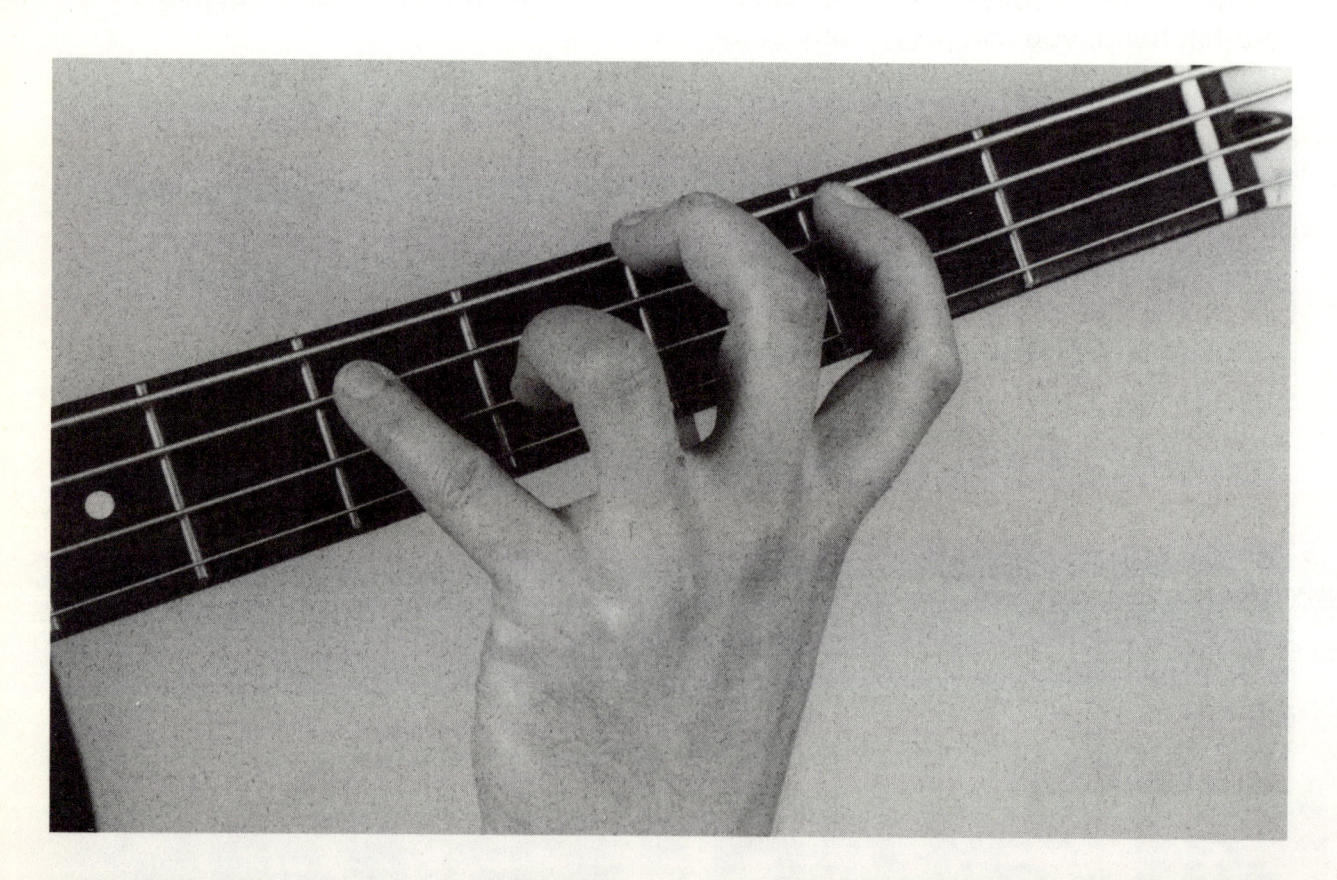

Walking Bass

Play this exercise, retaining the fingering pattern:
This is a typical Blues, Rhythm & Blues and Jazz style of playing. This technique is all about playing each quarter note in a measure.

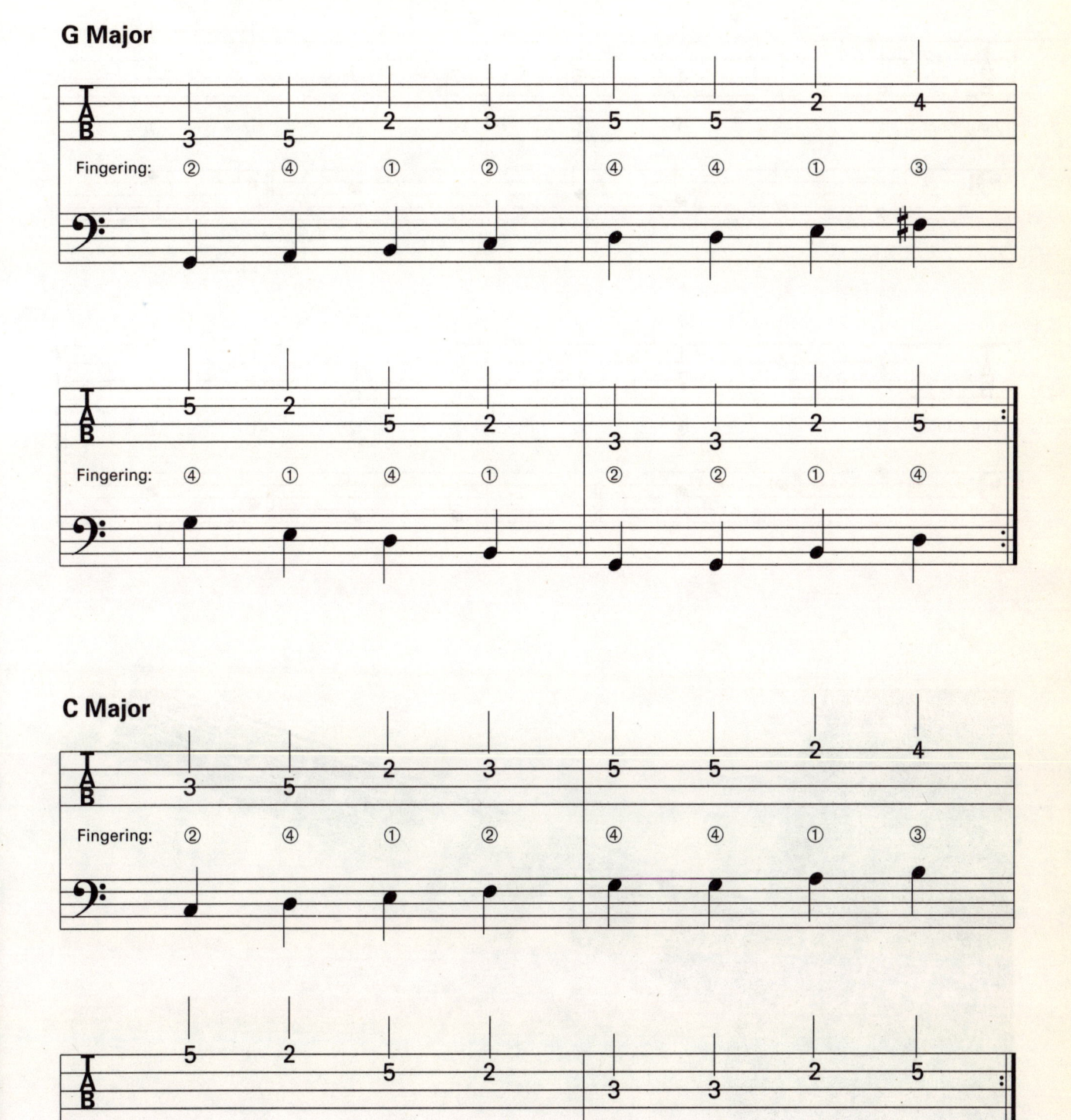

G Major

C Major

Now slide up two frets from the 3rd fret (= "G") to play A major.

The fingering always remains the same!

Rhythm and Blues

This note sequence is played without changing the position of your left hand.
In the beginning your fingers might hurt, but soon your left hand will feel very easy.

Here's the harmony pattern for the Blues in "G". (Every letter stands for one bar)

```
G   G   G   G
C   C   G   G
D   C   G   G
```

Let's play the following line together.

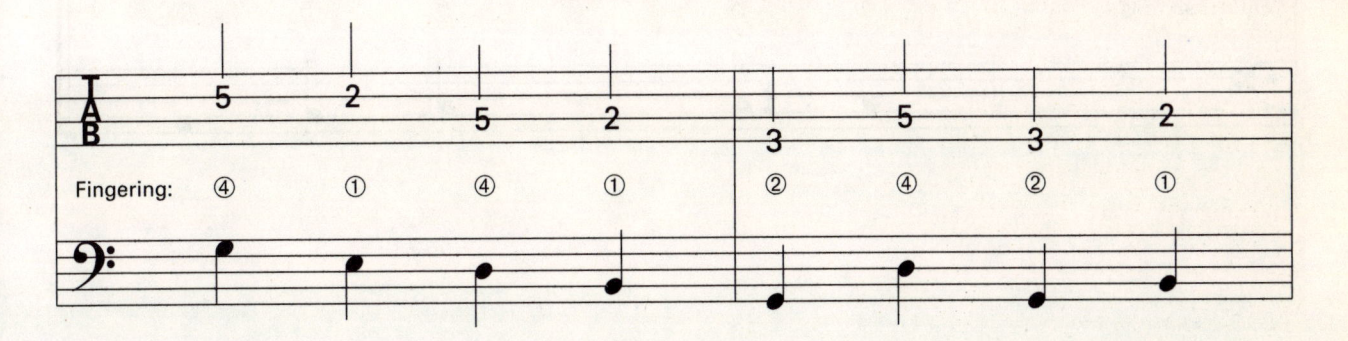

TAKE 11

TAB
3 5 3 2 | 5 2 3 4
Fingering: ② ④ ② ① | ④ ① ② ③
TAB
3 5 3 2 | 5 2 3 4
Fingering: ② ④ ② ① | ④ ① ② ③
TAB
5 2 4 5 | 3 2 0 3
Fingering: ④ ① ③ ④ | ② ① ⓪ ②
TAB
5 2 3 4 | 5 3 2 0
Fingering: ④ ① ② ③ | ④ ② ① ⓪

The House of the Rising Sun

In this example you are dealing with chord symbols for the first time.
I will tell you what they mean on the following pages. First, play the root notes of the following chord progression:

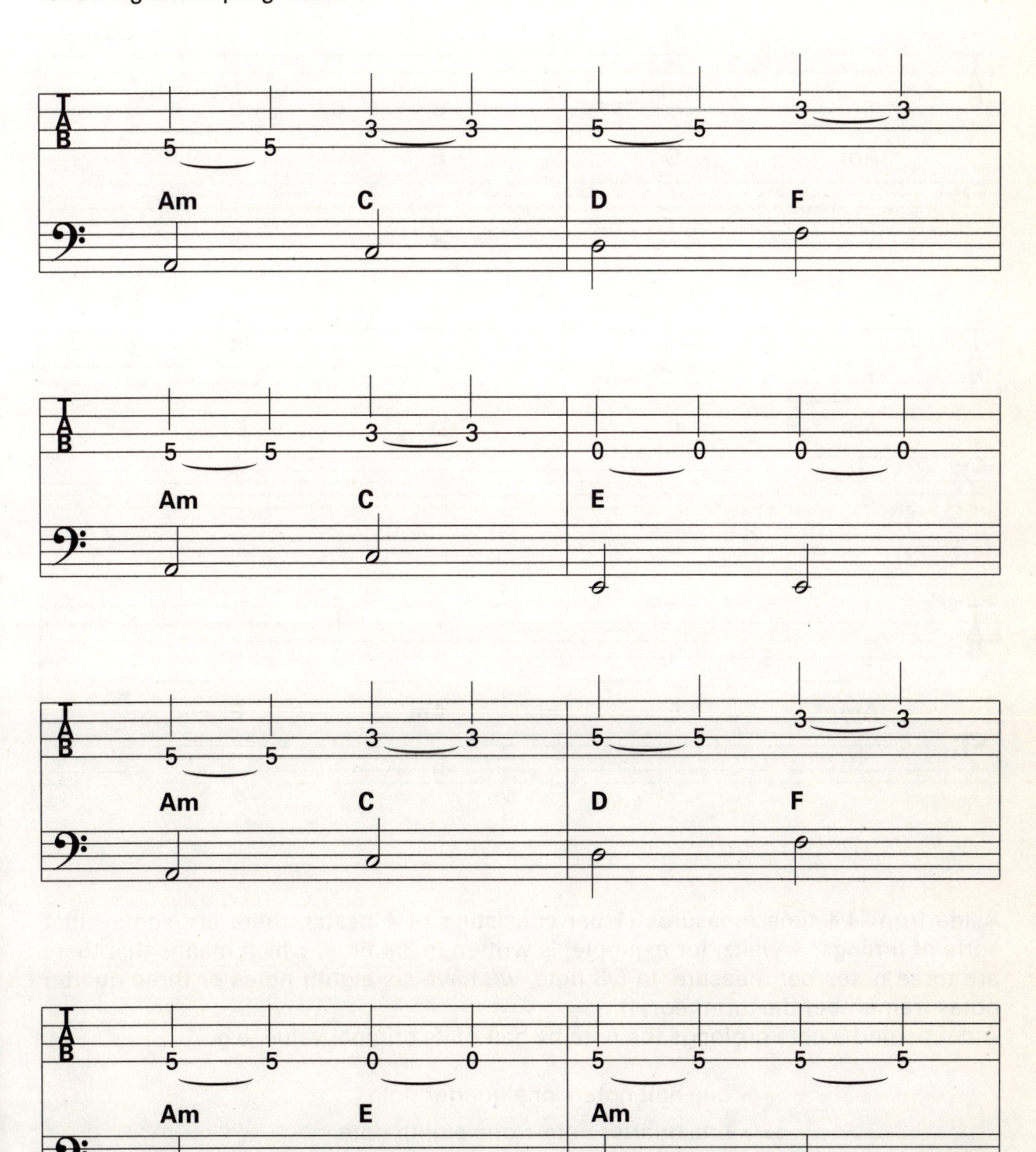

Aside from 4/4 time measures (1 bar consisting of 4 beats), there are some other sorts of timings. A waltz, for example, is written in 3/4 time, which means that there are three notes per measure. In 6/8 time, we have six eighth notes or three quarter notes (remember the tart theory!).
A dot behind a note prolongs the note by half of its original value, e.g.

𝅗𝅥. = one half note + one quarter note

♩. = one quarter note + one eighth note

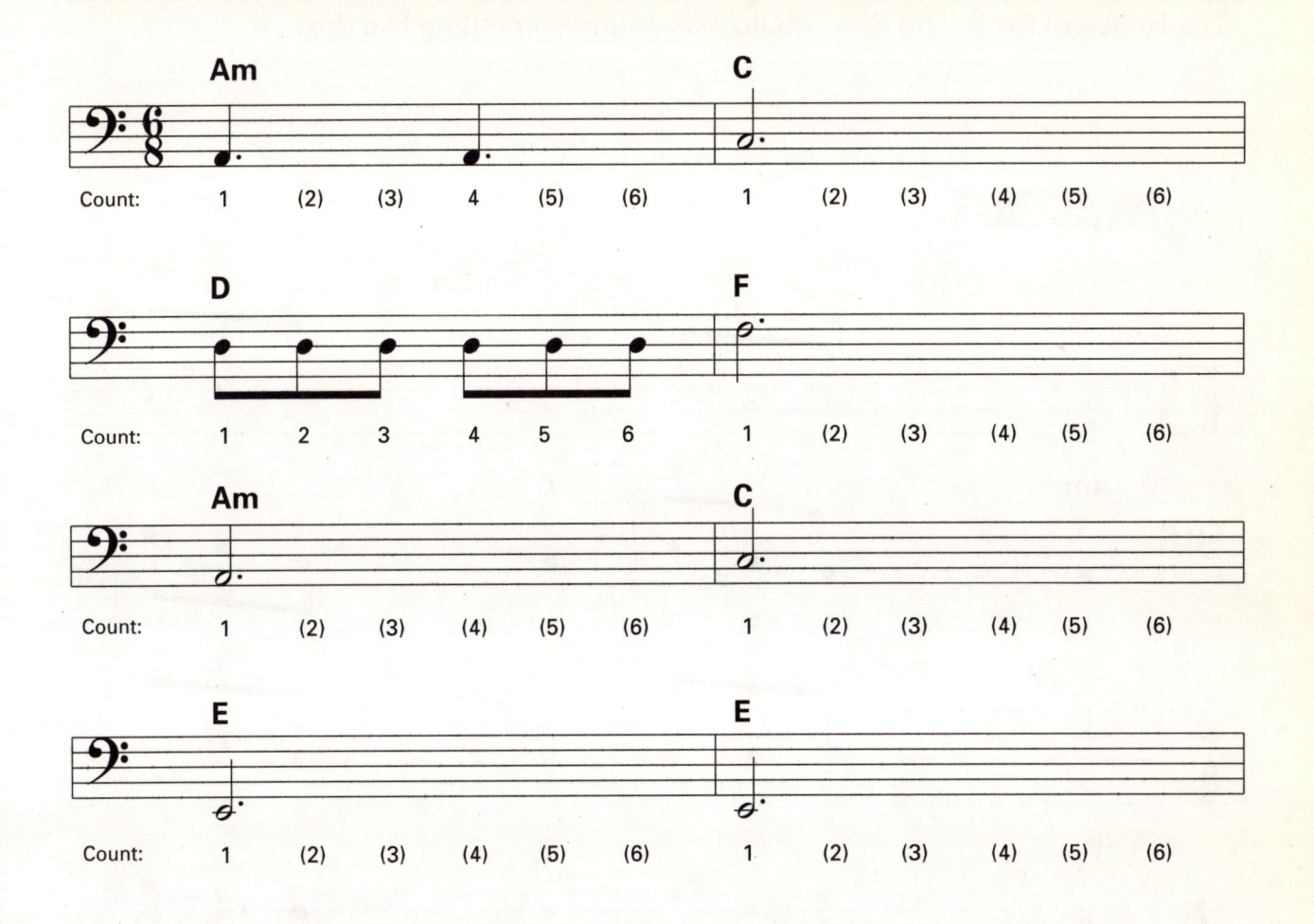

No bass player wants to simply play the root notes of the harmony. With these notes, which fit the respective harmonies, you can create a more interesting bass line:

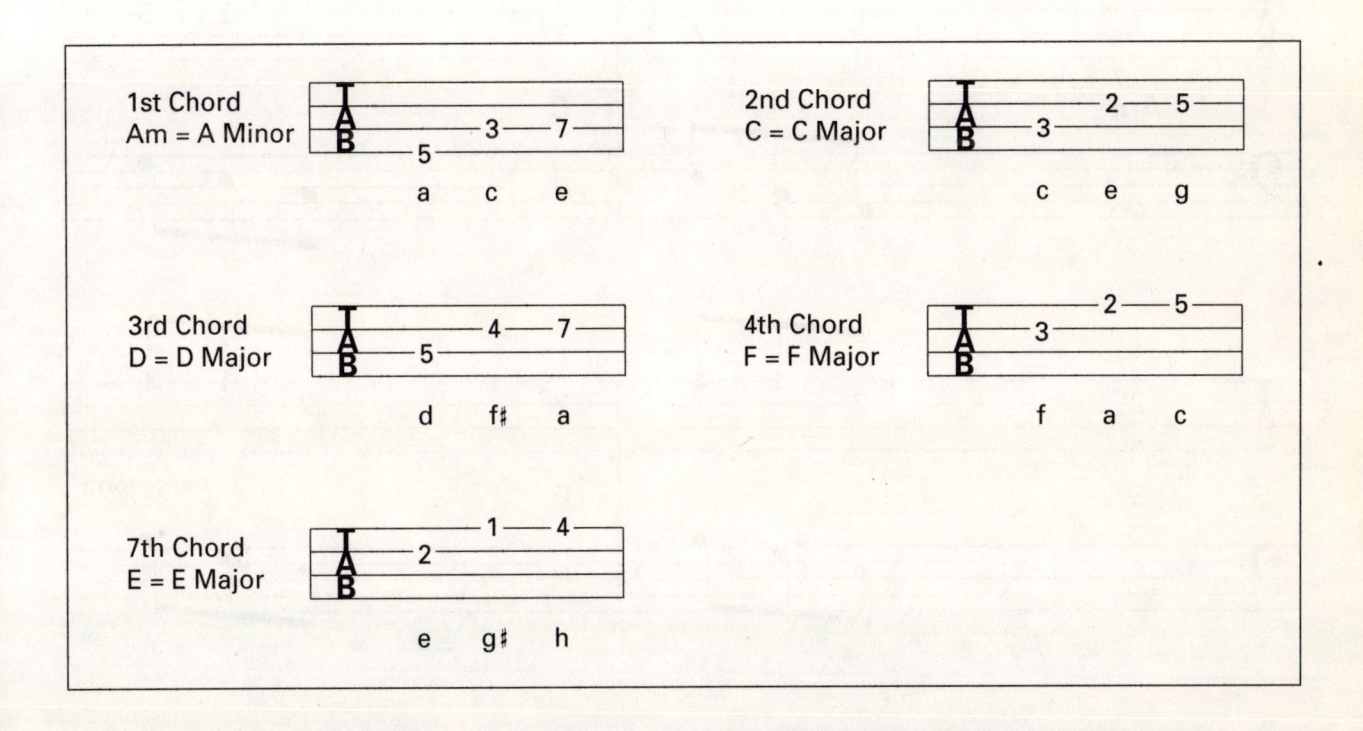

1st Chord
Am = A Minor
a c e

2nd Chord
C = C Major
c e g

3rd Chord
D = D Major
d f# a

4th Chord
F = F Major
f a c

7th Chord
E = E Major
e g# h

"The House of the Rising Sun" could also sound something like this:

TAKE 12

Count: 1 (2) (3) 4 5 6

and so forth

Harmony

... "in passing"

Major and minor don't only exist in life; you also have to deal chordally with them on a regular basis as a bass player.

A Major Chord

Chords normally consist of at least three notes.

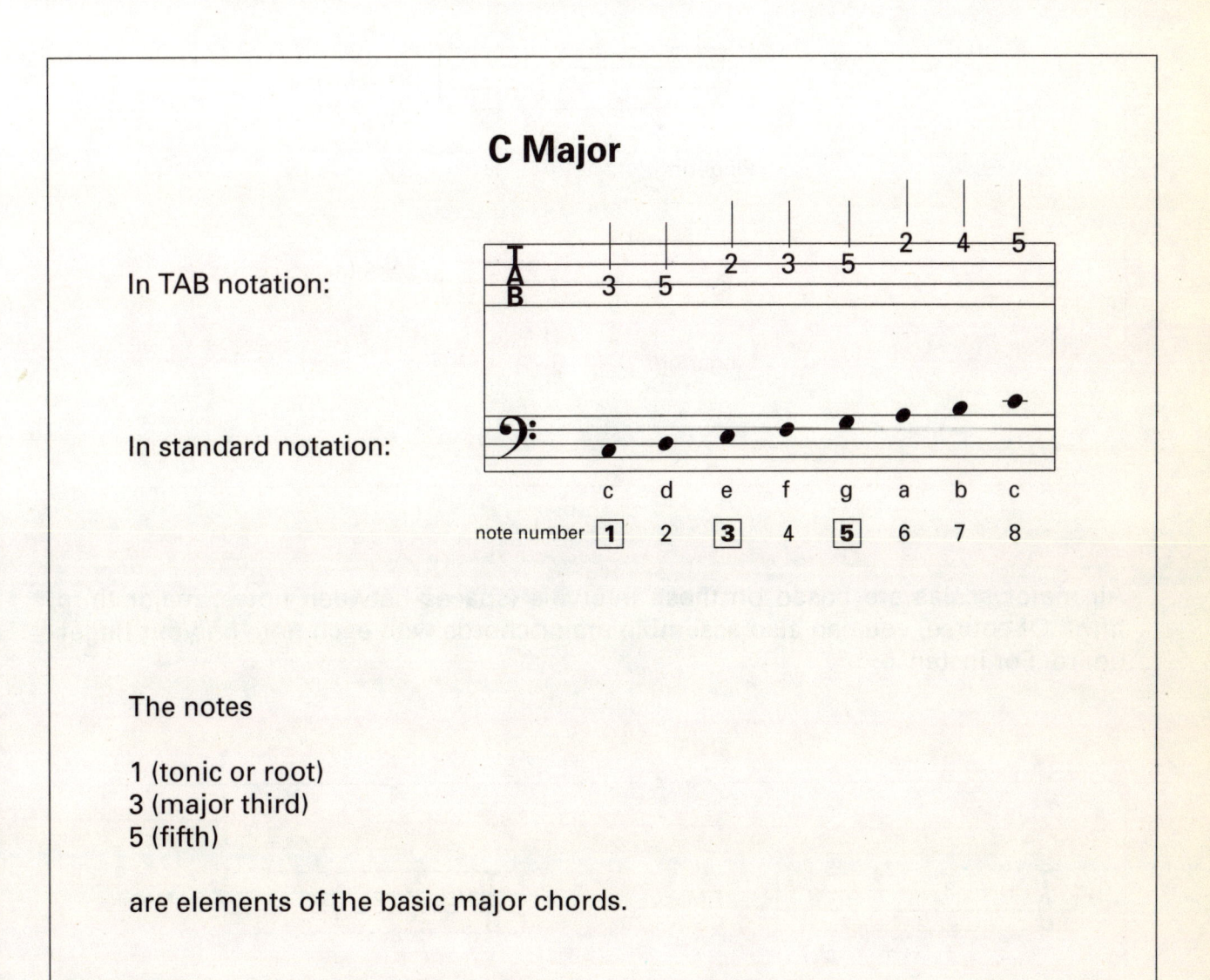

C Major

In TAB notation:

In standard notation:

note number 1 2 3 4 5 6 7 8

The notes

1 (tonic or root)
3 (major third)
5 (fifth)

are elements of the basic major chords.

Important! The fingering remains the same.

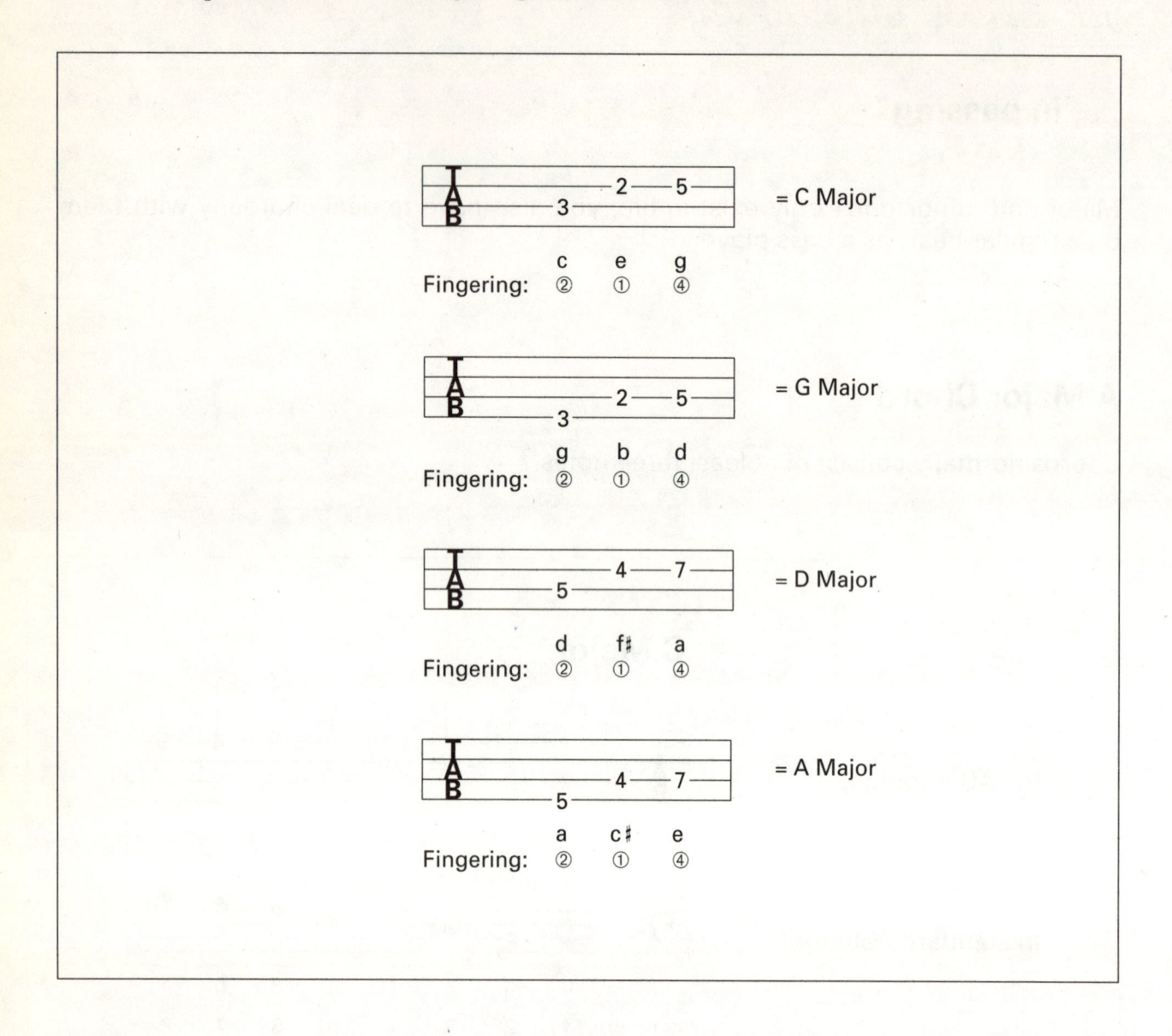

```
T
A ———2———5—
B ——3————————   = C Major
```
Fingering: c ②   e ①   g ④

```
T
A ———2———5—
B —3——————      = G Major
```
Fingering: g ②   b ①   d ④

```
T
A ———4———7—
B ——5————————   = D Major
```
Fingering: d ②   f♯ ①   a ④

```
T
A ———4———7—
B —5——————      = A Major
```
Fingering: a ②   c♯ ①   e ④

All major scales are based on these intervals (spaces between notes: major third, fifth). Of course, you can also assemble major chords with each note on your fingerboard. For instance:

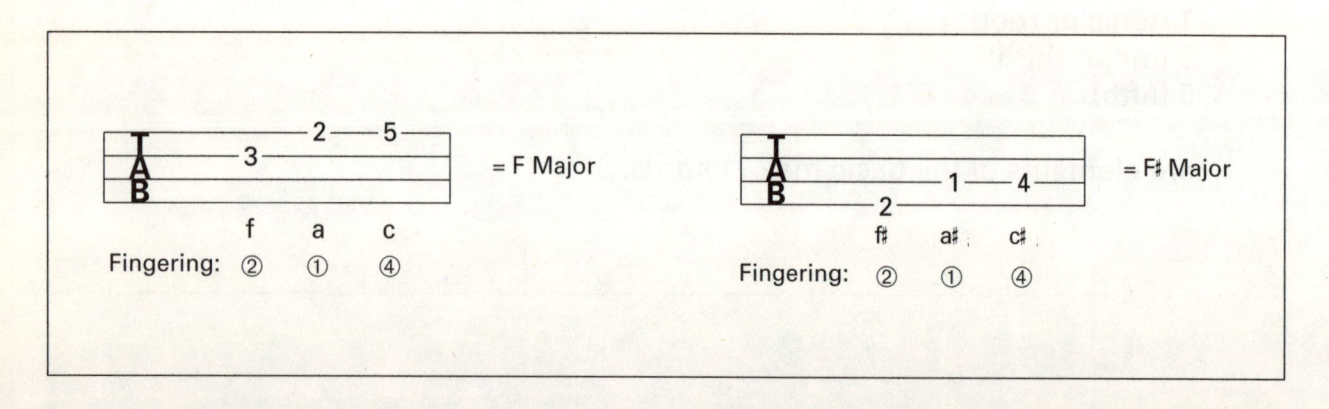

```
T
A ——2———5—
B —3—————       = F Major
```
Fingering: f ②   a ①   c ④

```
T
A ———1———4—
B —2——————      = F♯ Major
```
Fingering: f♯ ②   a♯ ①   c♯ ④

Find out the following chords and write them down in TAB notation:

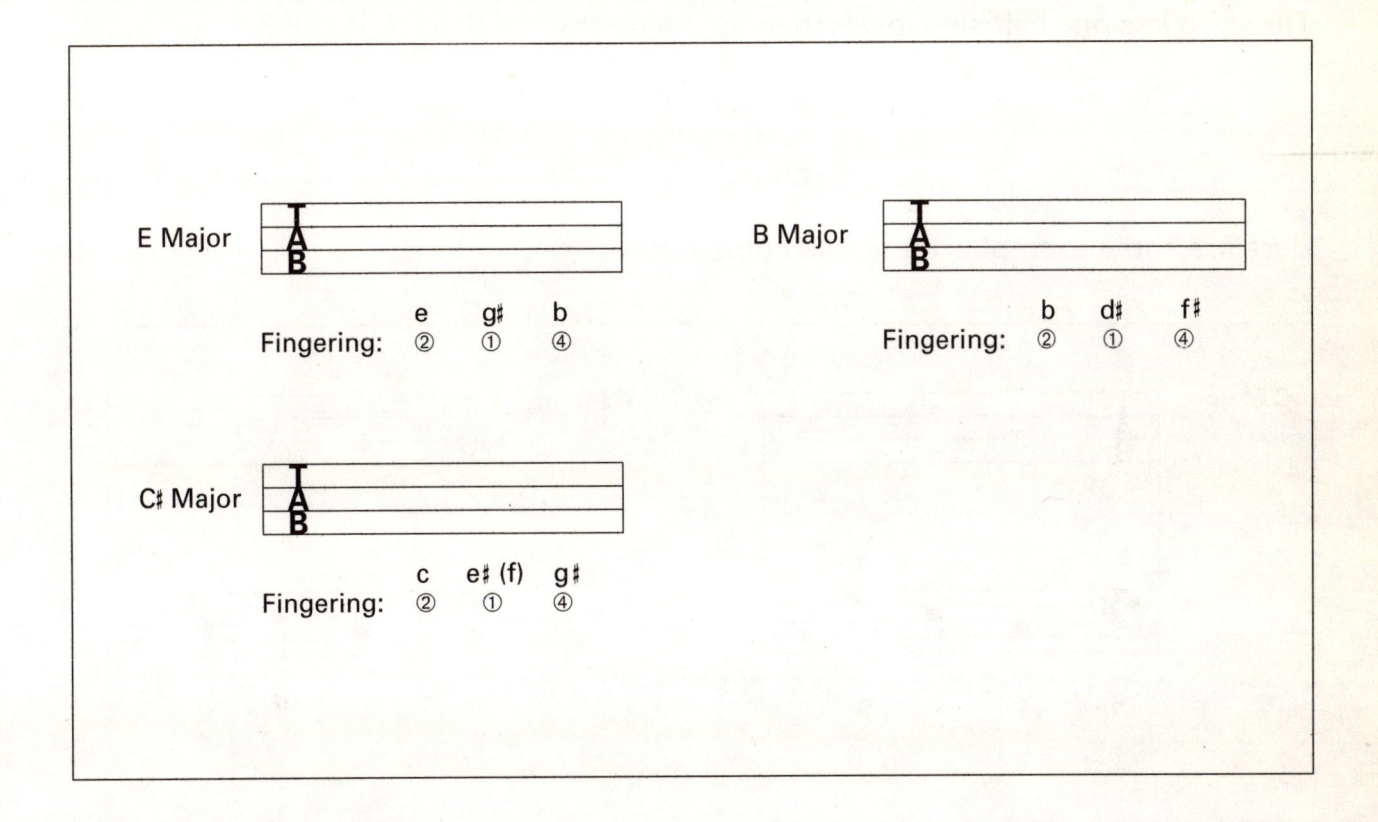

E Major

```
T|―――――――――――
A|―――――――――――
B|―――――――――――
```

           e   g♯   b
Fingering: ②   ①   ④

B Major

```
T|―――――――――――
A|―――――――――――
B|―――――――――――
```

           b   d♯   f♯
Fingering: ②   ①   ④

C♯ Major

```
T|―――――――――――
A|―――――――――――
B|―――――――――――
```

           c   e♯ (f)   g♯
Fingering: ②   ①   ④

Minor Chords

The only difference between a major and a minor chord is tone number 3 (the third). The third lies one half step lower than the major third and we thus call it minor third.

                      1 (tonic, root)
                      3 (minor third)
                      5 (fifth)

Here are some examples for you to compare:

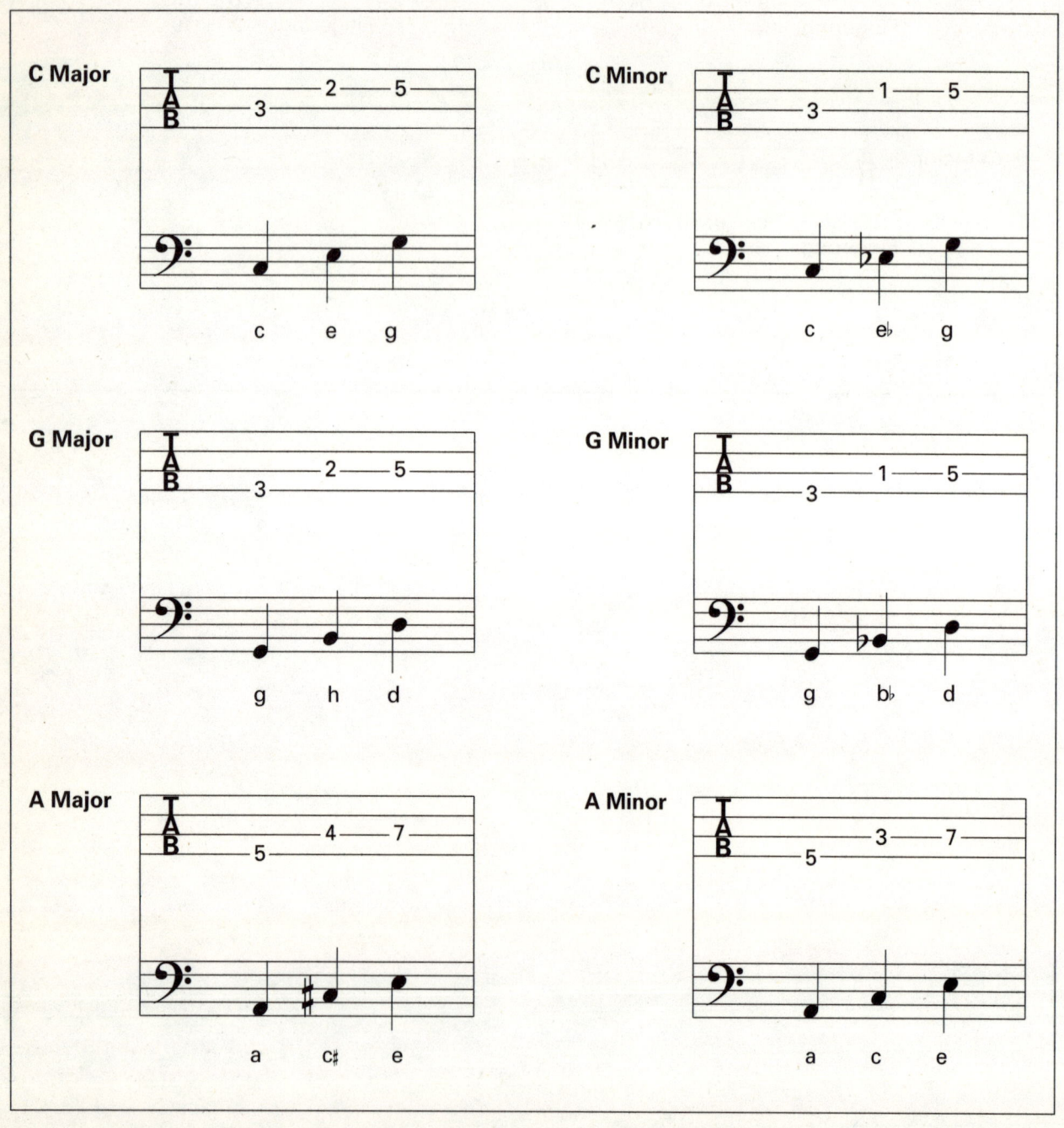

O.K.! Enough of the theory. In the next chapter we'll continue with some bass lines.

Chapter 4

Soul Music

Typical Soul bass lines now follow.
A little hint: Listen to the following takes very closely. This is very important, in order to get the right rhythmic feeling.

The **ties** indicate that the note is held longer, i.e., you play the first note but not the second one.

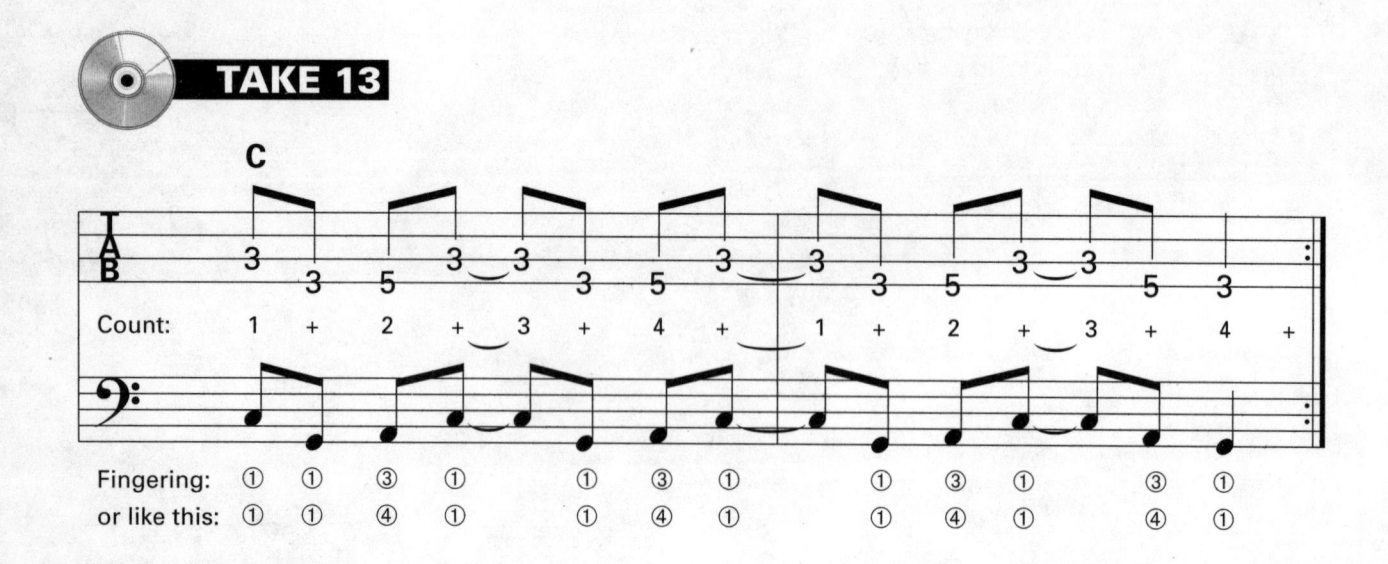

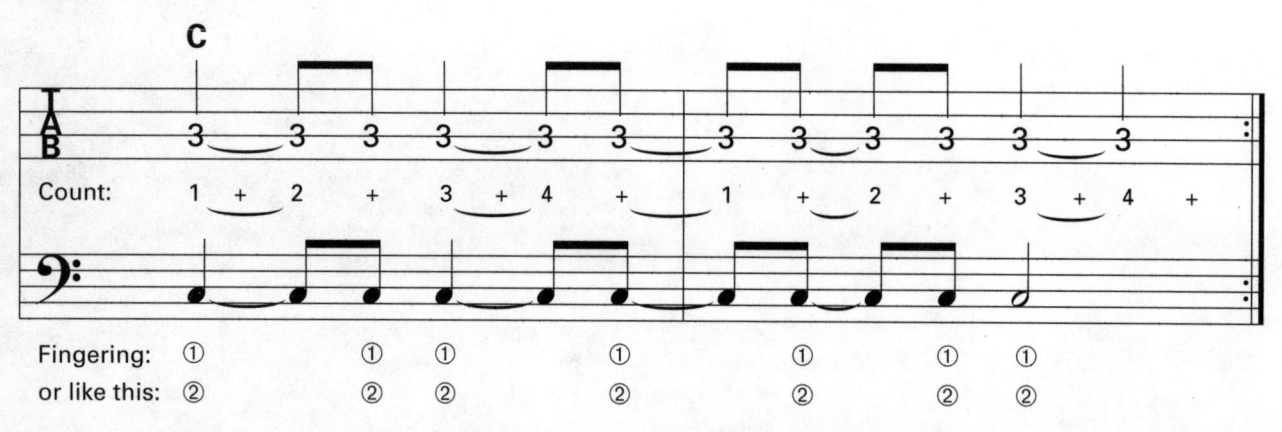

TAKE 13

TAKE 14

Try using different fingerings. Each one feels somewhat different. Choose the simpler ones in the beginning and then practice the harder ones. This will strengthen and train the precision of your fingers.
It looks worse than it is! More on this on the following pages.

TAKE 15

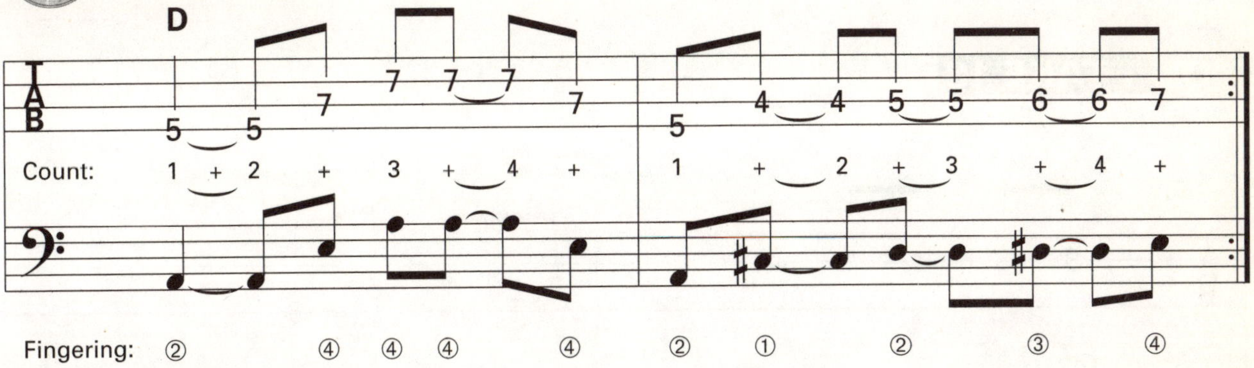

TAKE 16

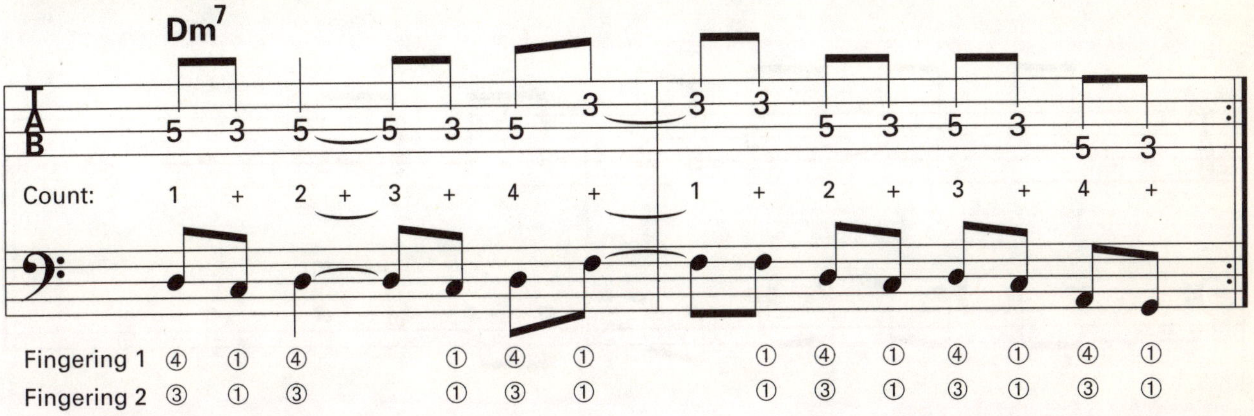

TAKE 17

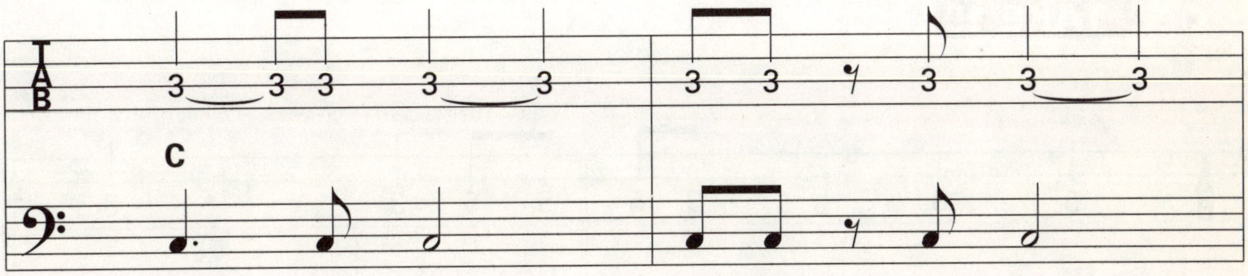

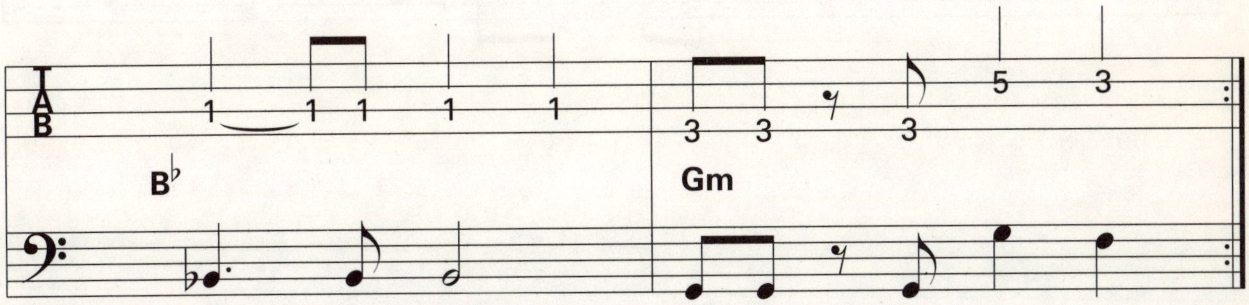

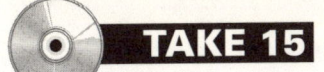

Bass lines do not necessarily have to start with a root note.

TAKE 18

TAKE 19

The bass line you've just played took you another step into understanding harmony. The following example shows you which notes to play when you read, say, a C7 chord symbol.

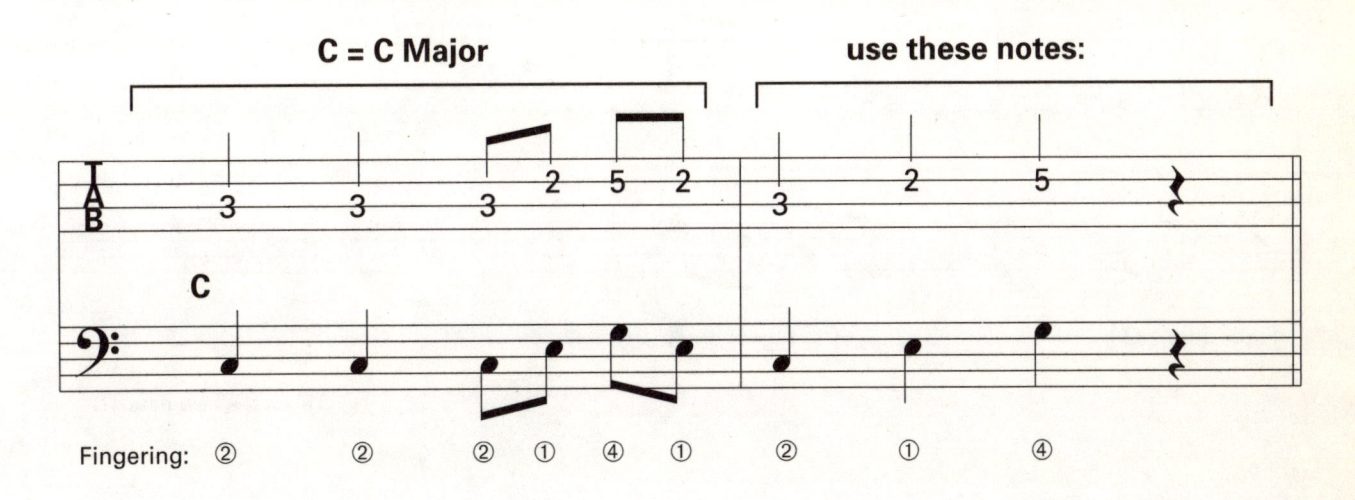

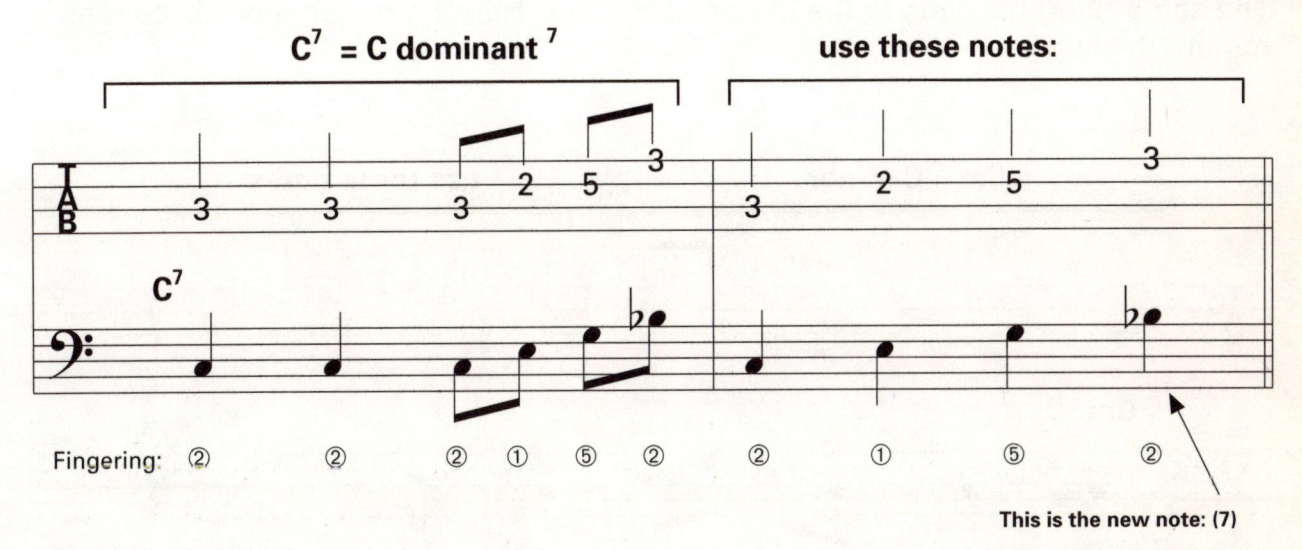

C = C Major — use these notes:

(musical notation with tab and bass clef; chord symbol C; Fingering: ② ② ② ① ④ ① | ② ① ④)

C⁷ = C dominant ⁷ — use these notes:

(musical notation with tab and bass clef; chord symbol C⁷; Fingering: ② ② ② ① ⑤ ② | ② ① ⑤ ②)

This is the new note: (♭7)

How to play the notes of G and G7

The fingering and the distance between the notes remain the same, you only have to memorize them once. No matter which root note on the two lower strings you start from, you will immediately make out the right notes.

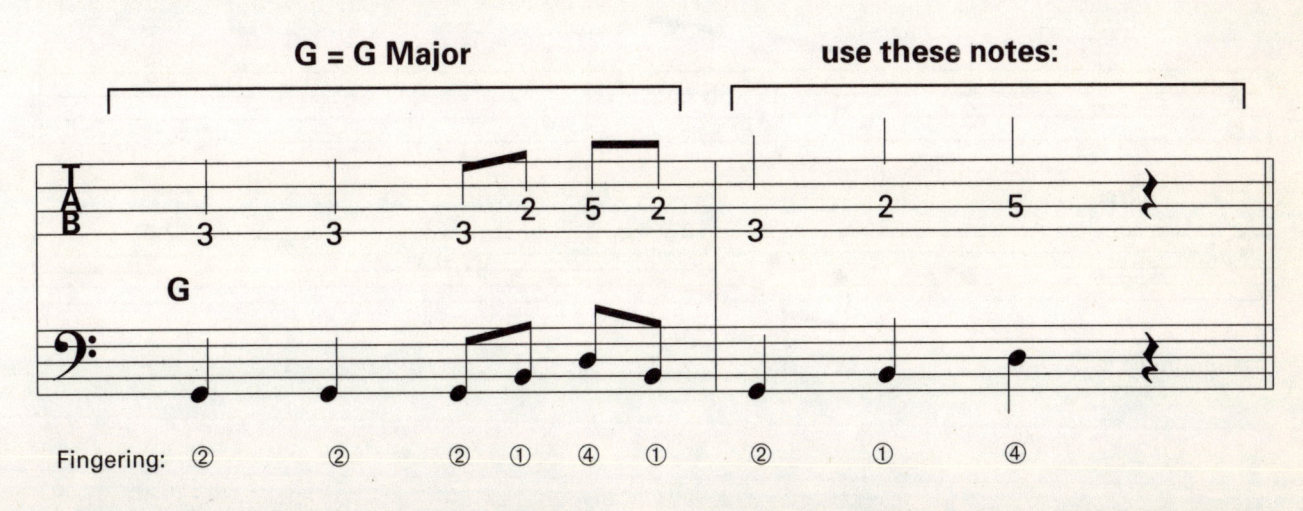

G = G Major — use these notes:

(musical notation with tab and bass clef; chord symbol G; Fingering: ② ② ② ① ④ ① | ② ① ④)

73

G^7 = G dominant ^{7} use these notes:

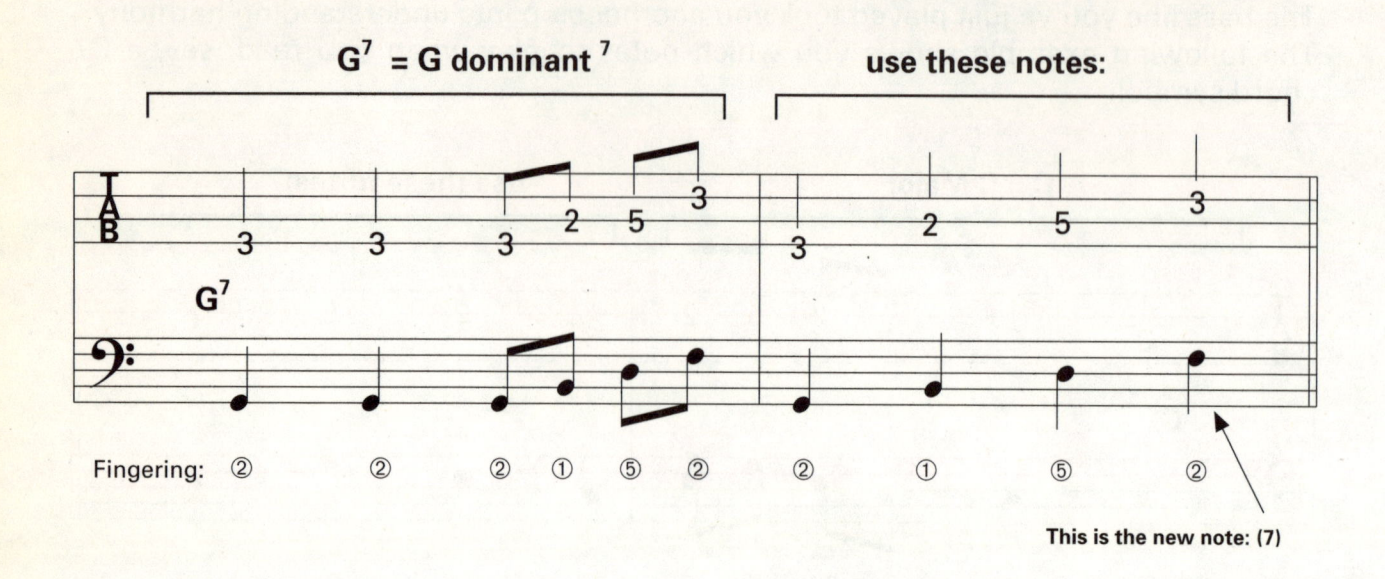

This is the new note: (7)

The same thing happens to the minor harmonies. Here's a minor chord becoming a minor 7th chord:

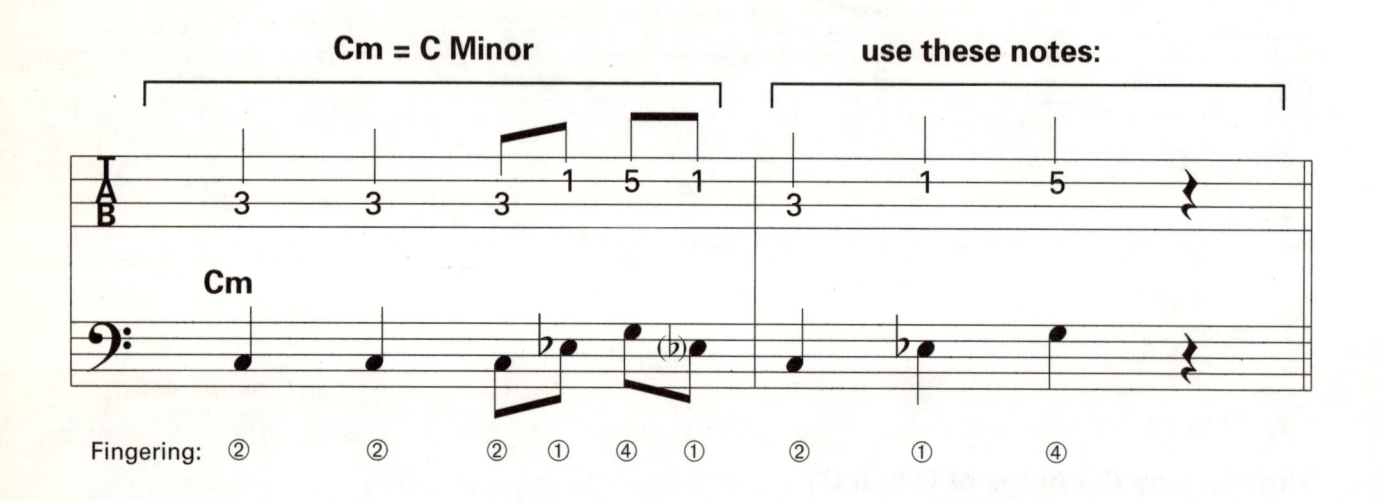

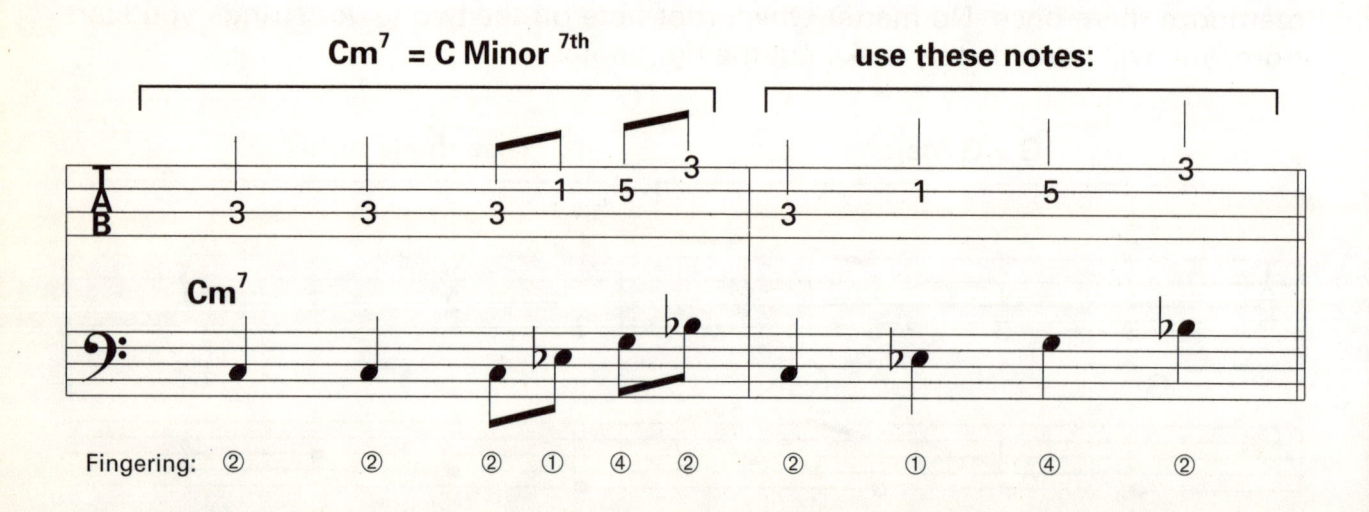

Cm = C Minor   use these notes:

Cm^7 = C Minor ^{7th} use these notes:

Once again, we conclude:

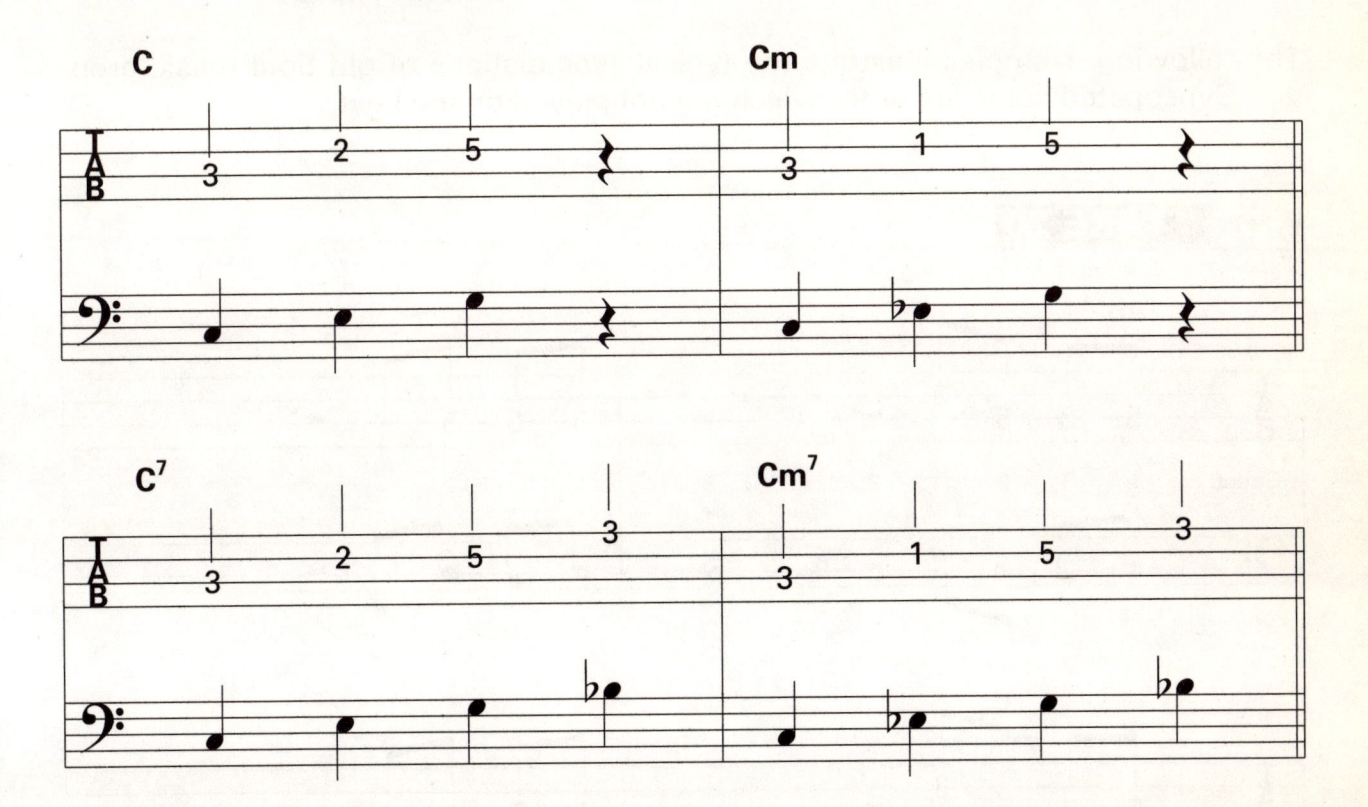

Soulbrothers Delight

The following examples illustrate the typical syncopations of old Soul music grooves. Syncopated notes are notes which are not played on the beat.

TAKE 20

TAKE 21

TAKE 22

77

Memphis Soul

TAKE 23

Rhythm and Blues

TAKE 24

Otis Blue

Mustang Annie

TAKE 25

Alternating Bass Notes

This is a simple, yet very popular, style of playing.

Carnival or Country?

Dixieland or Samba?

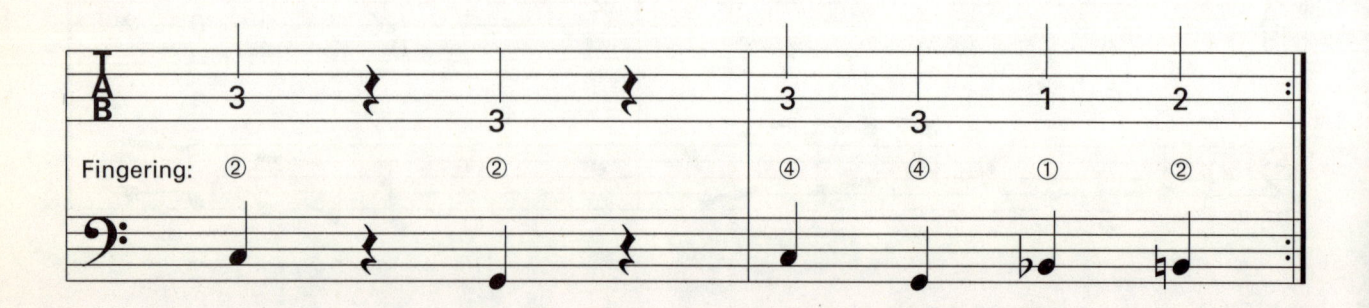

Classical or Pop?

Triad's Rock

Welcome to "triplet" feel. Triplets arise by dividing the value of a note into three notes of equal value. Triplets are identified by the figure "3" written above or below the notes. Quarter notes are the result of the division of half notes.

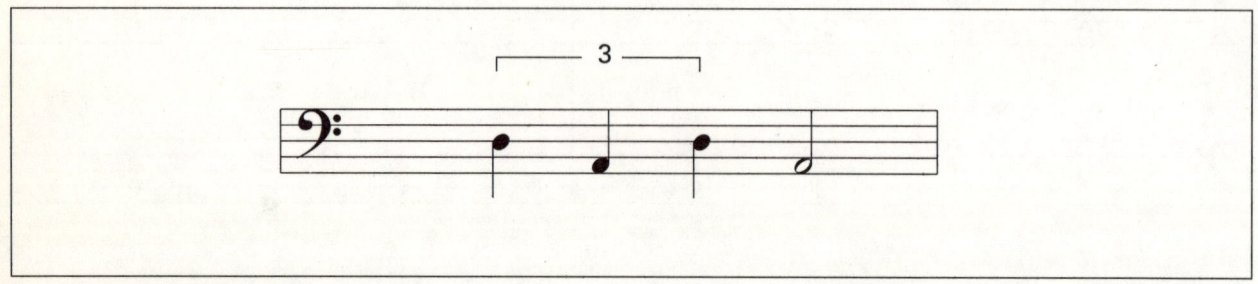

By dividing half notes by two you get quarter notes. By dividing a half note by three you get a quarter-note triplet. You can do the same thing with quarter notes, which become eighth-note triplets when divided by three.
Following this pattern, a whole note becomes a half-note triplet.

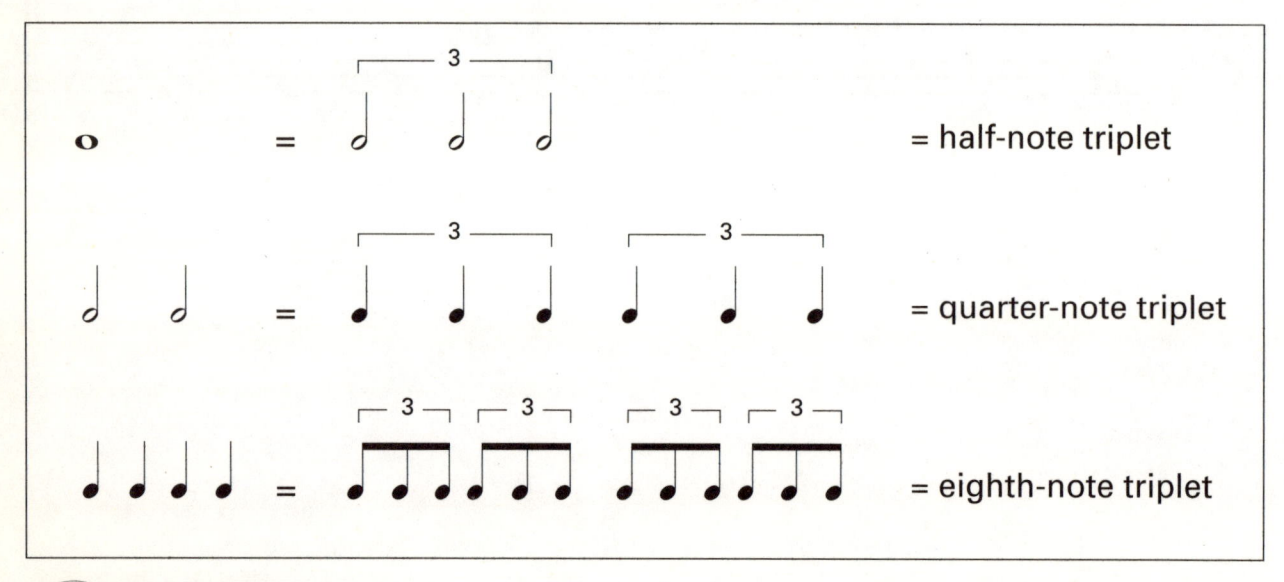

TAKE 26

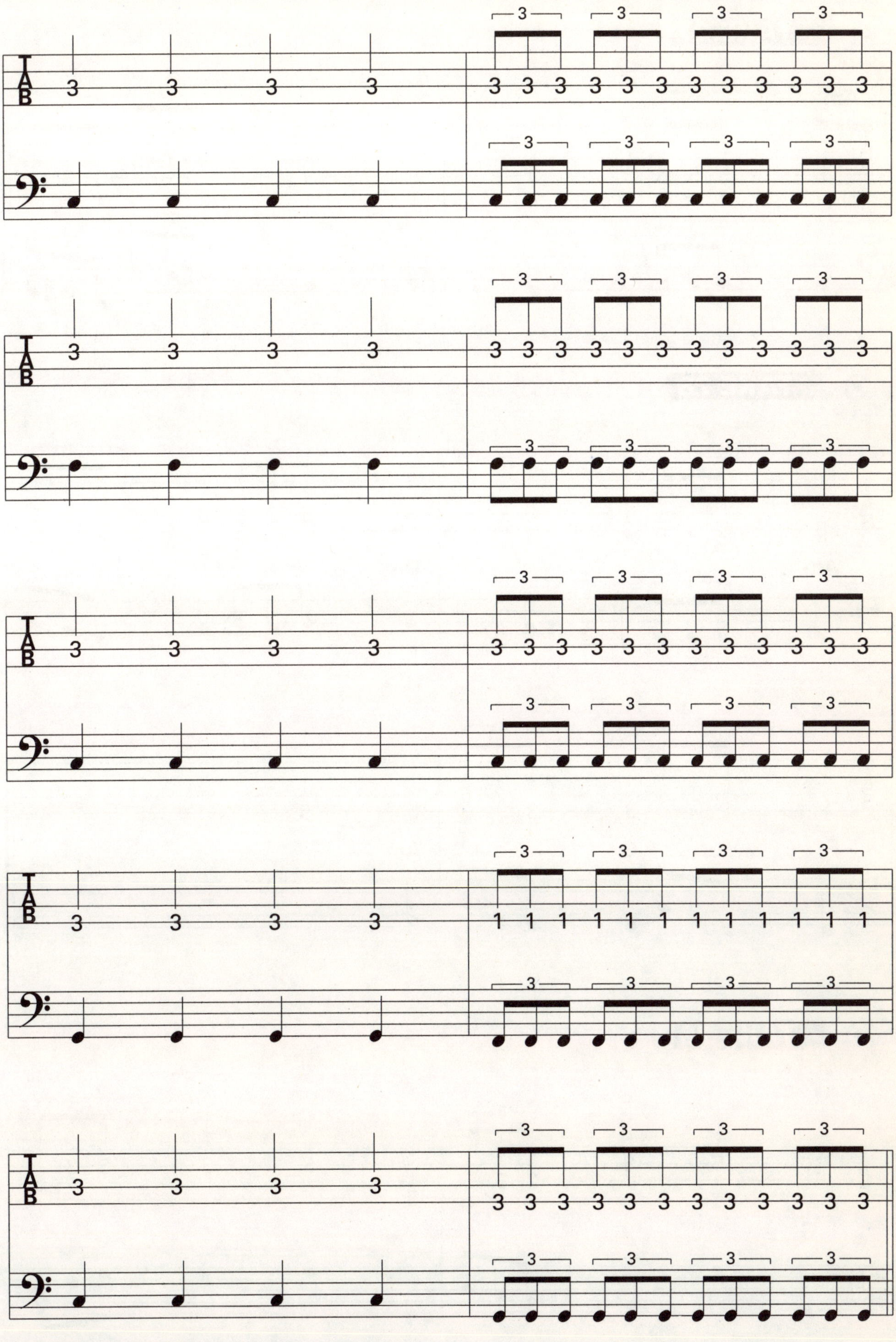

86

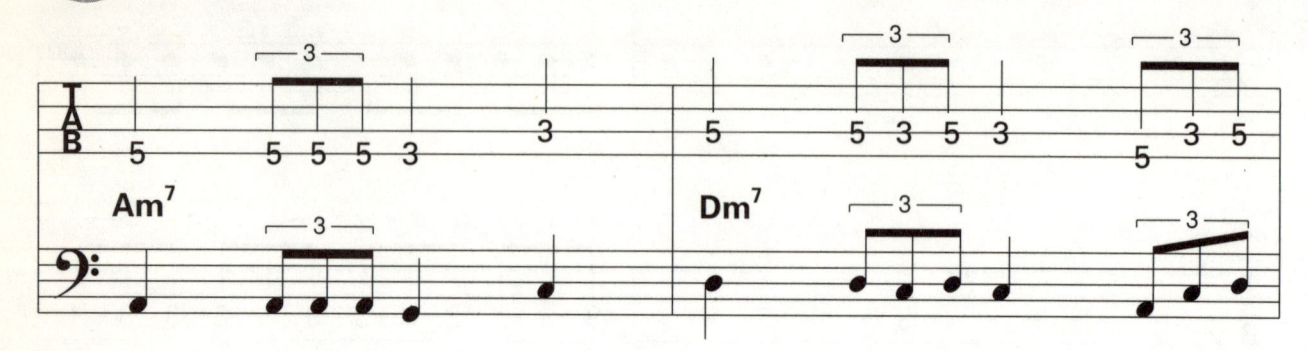

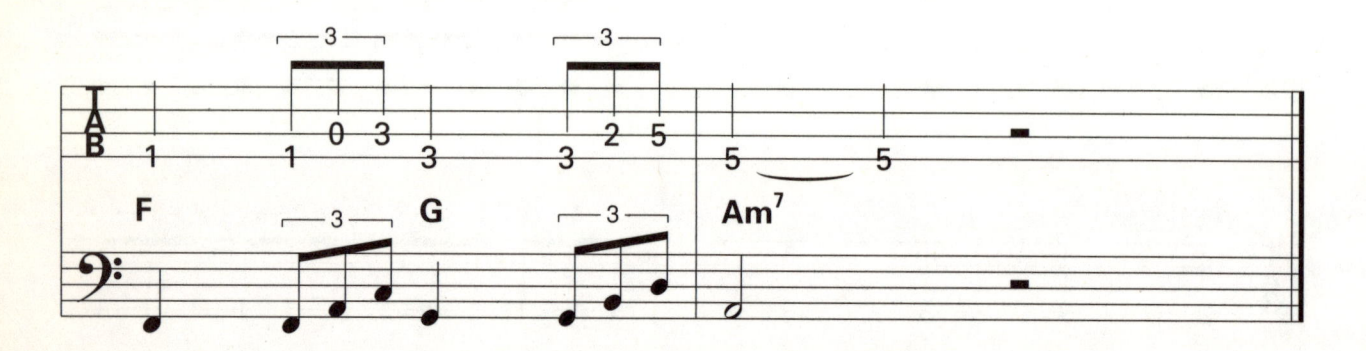

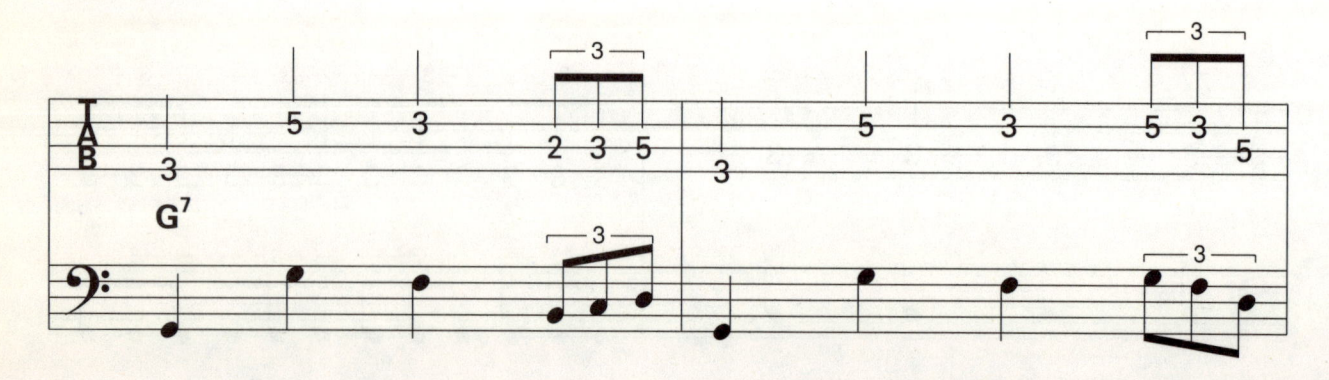

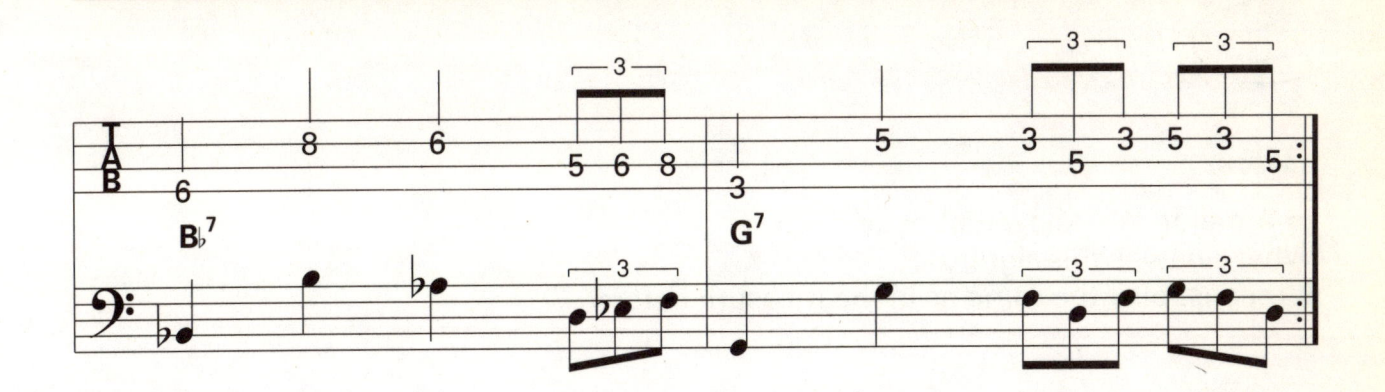

Shuffle

A whole new variation shows itself when you replace the middle eighth note of the eighth-note triplet with a rest.

TAKE 30

Shuffle Blues

In A major. You know it already.
What's new is this sign: 𝄎
It means: play the same as in the measure before.

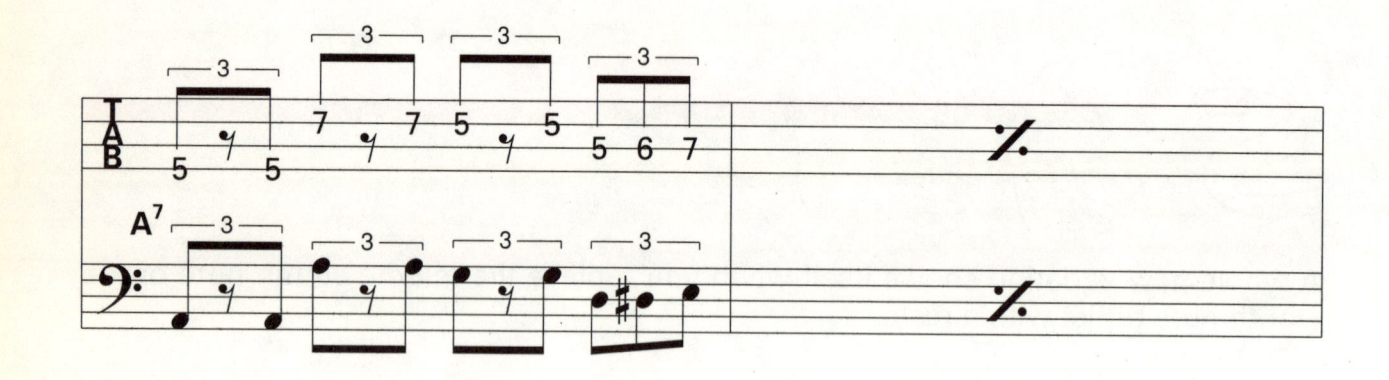

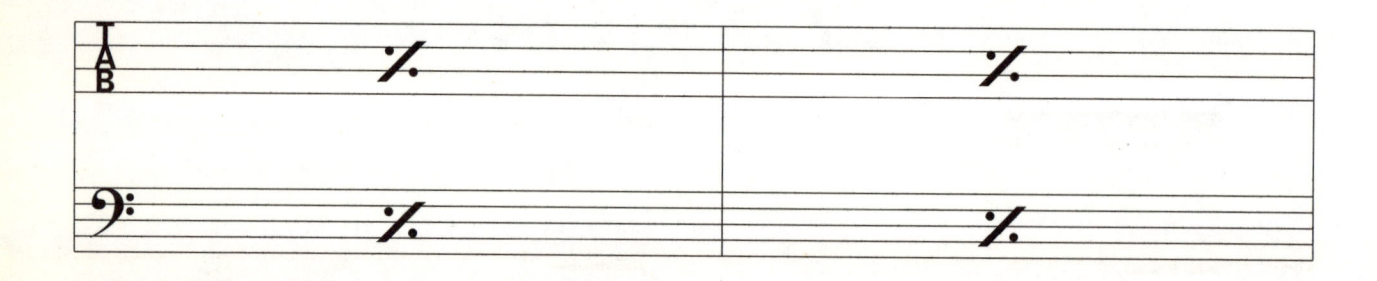

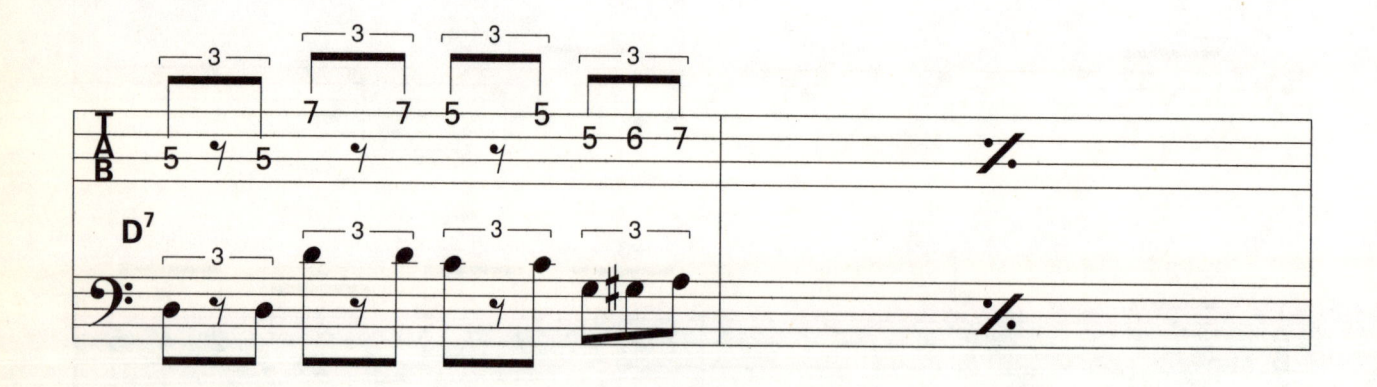

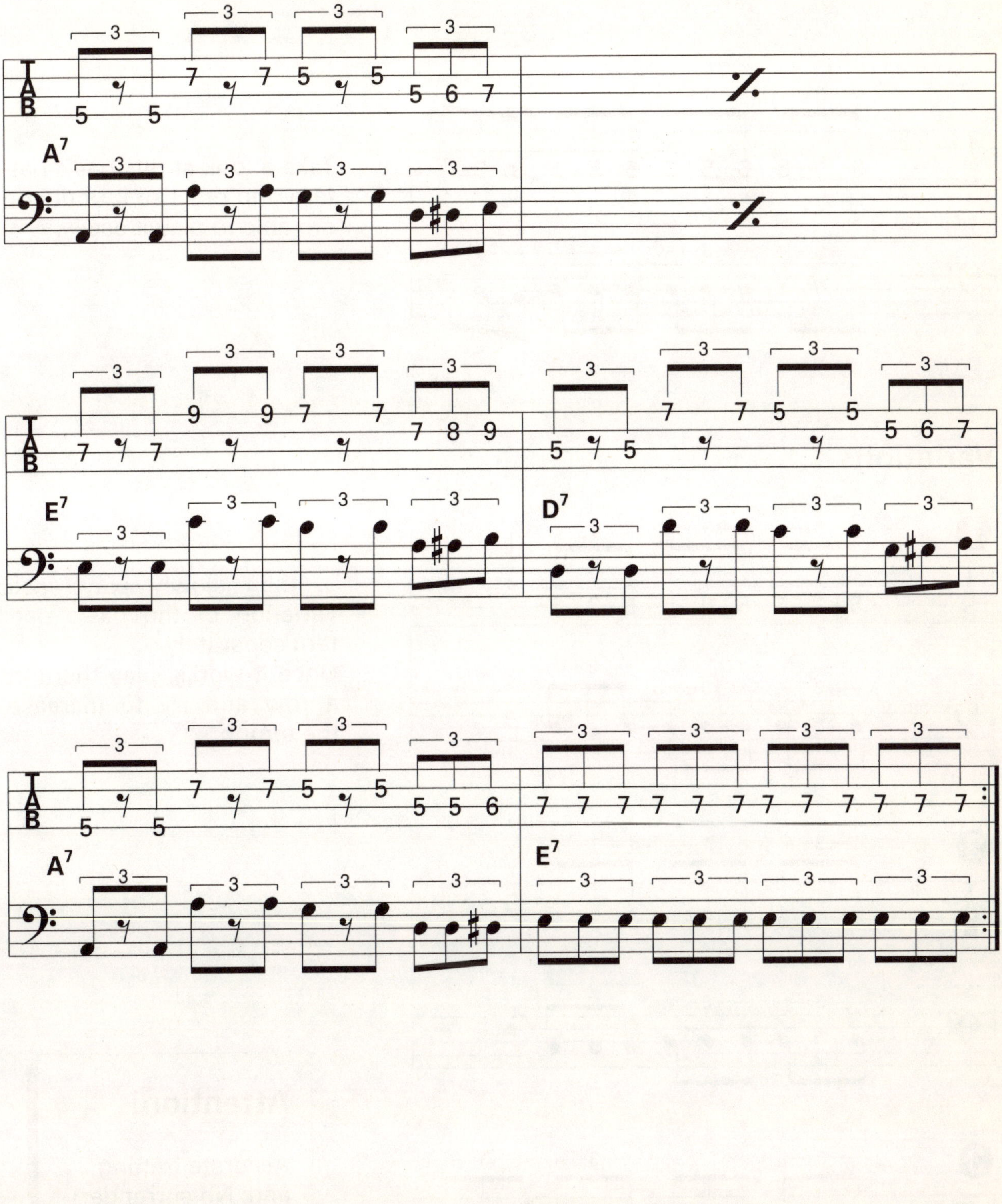
A7
E7
D7
A7
E7

Heavy Rock Shuffle

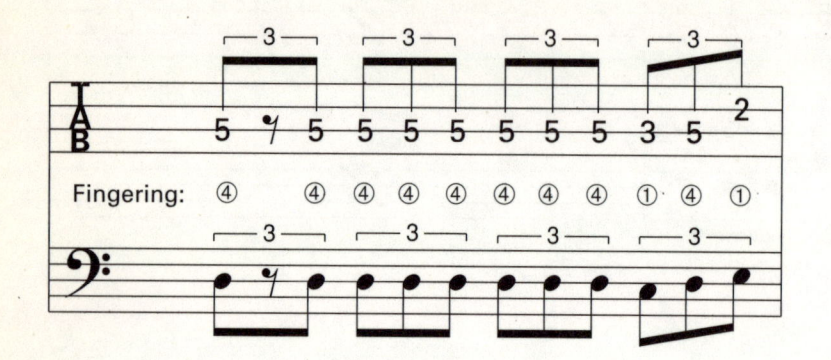

Fingering: ④ ④ ④ ④ ④ ④ ④ ④ ① ④ ①

Take a look at this basic pattern and practise it until you are able to play it easily.

Variations

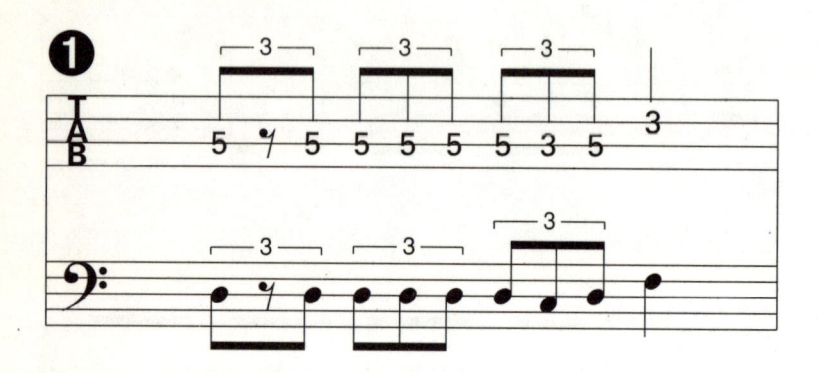

❶

... then slowly play each variation of the basic pattern separately.
Once it works, play them in a row and try to increase the tempo.

❷

❸

Attention!

Accurate fretting and: No surrender!

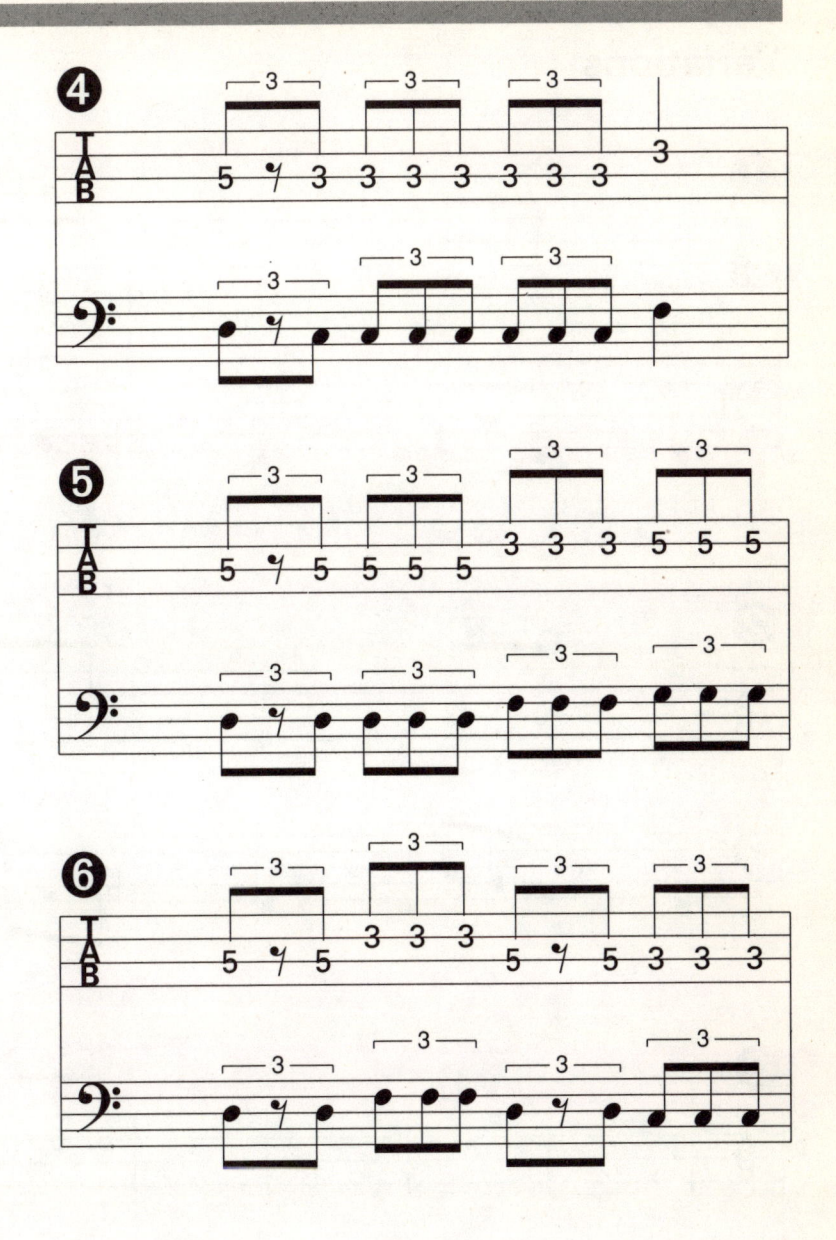

And heavy

we'll continue. Again, let's start off with the basic pattern. Try playing faster this time. If this doesn't sound accurate, start over again more slowly. Then gradually raise the tempo again.

TAKE 31

Variations

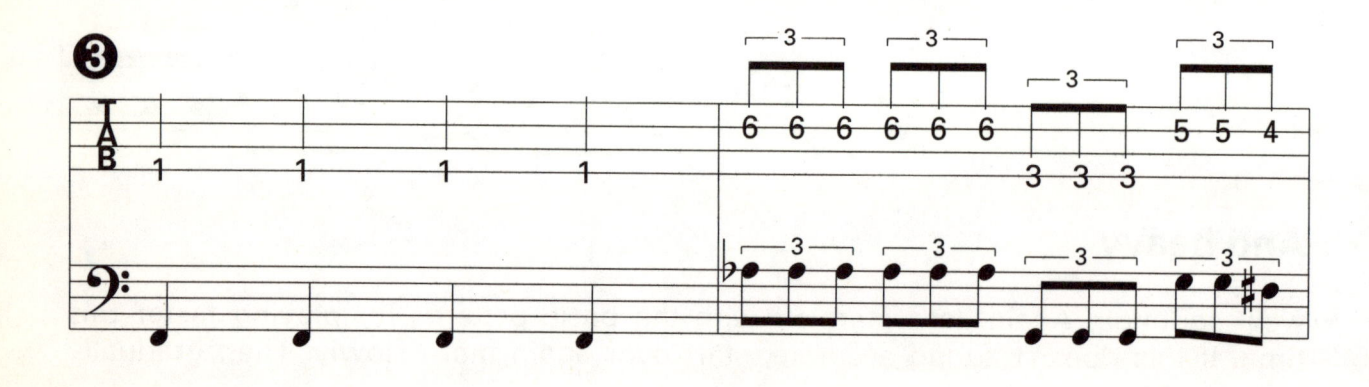

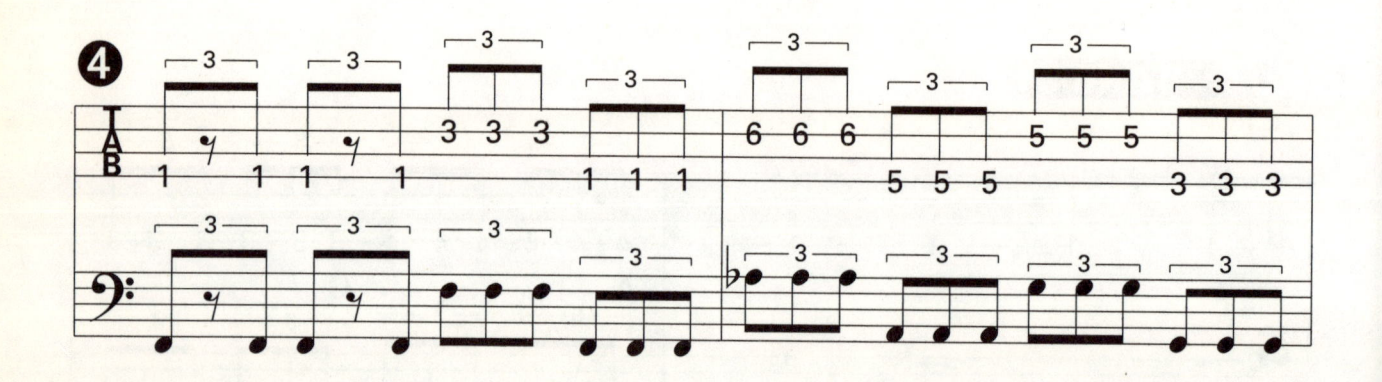

Wave Rock Licks

Licks are short melody lines and patterns.
Play all notes short (staccato), except the tied ones (legato).

TAKE 34

Chapter 5

Rock is, in most cases, a very basic style of music. Many times, especially the bass lines are very simply structured. If you listen closely enough, you recognize some little tricks which make them sound alive. I would like to prove my point with this song that consists of one and the same basic chord change throughout the piece. Here's the simple version:

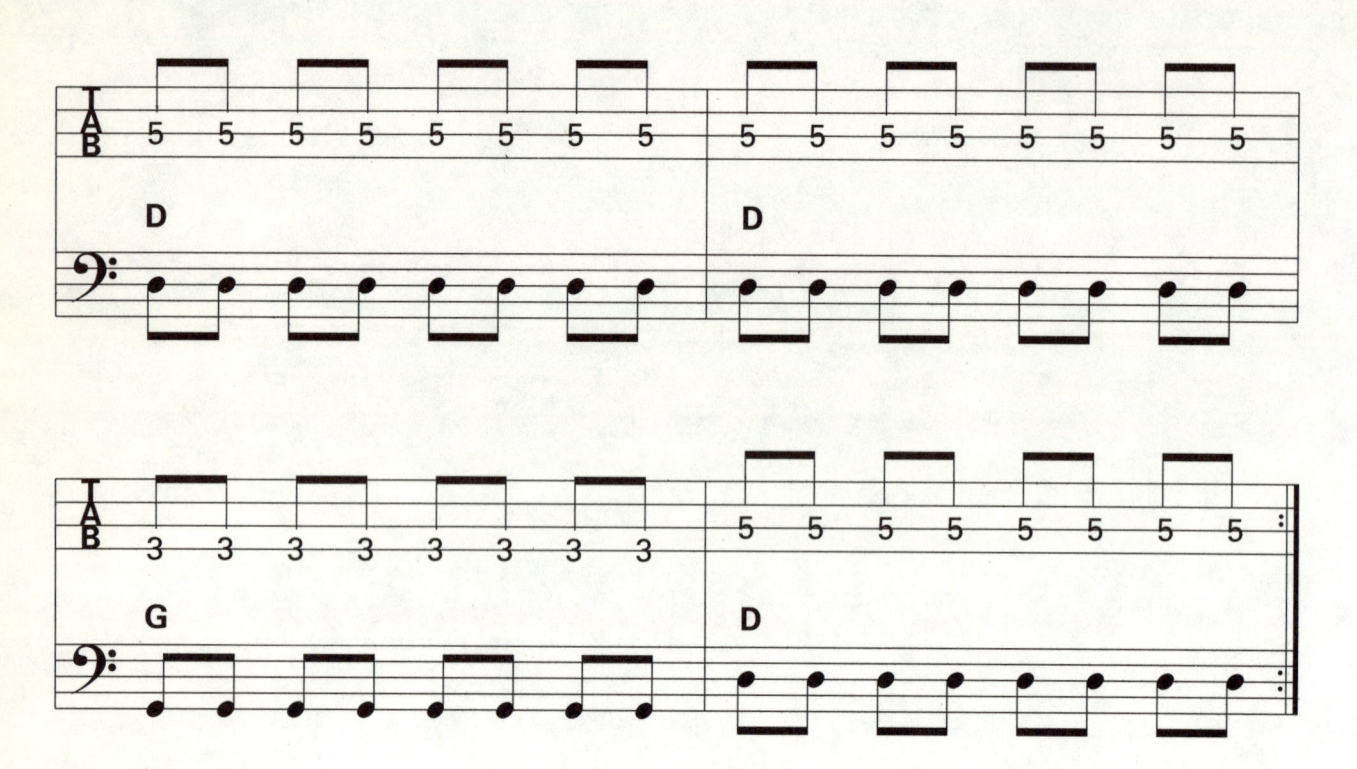

In the verse and the chorus you are playing eighth notes in order to create a solid foundation for the groove.

One means of "coloring" the arrangement is a slide, which simply means sliding from one note to the other. In standard notation a slide is indicated by a wavy line. This technique is often used to effectively combine two notes.

With the slide in our example, you start two half notes (i.e. two frets) down from the root note and then slide up to the root note.

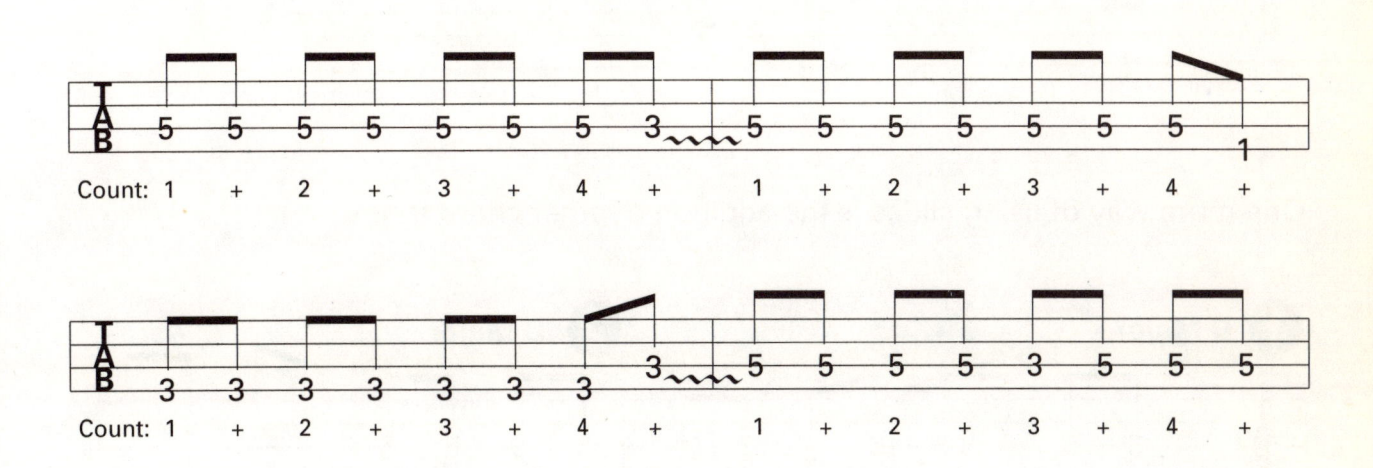

A slide does not always have to include two notes:

Attention! In bar 2 and 4 the slide is a little harder to do. You start with your index finger on the A-string (note D) and then slide up until you can reach the D on the D-string with your little finger. This goes pretty fast. If the time's too short, simply interrupt your slide. Let all notes ring as long as possible, in order to make them sound as wide as possible.

Upbeats are another application of slides:

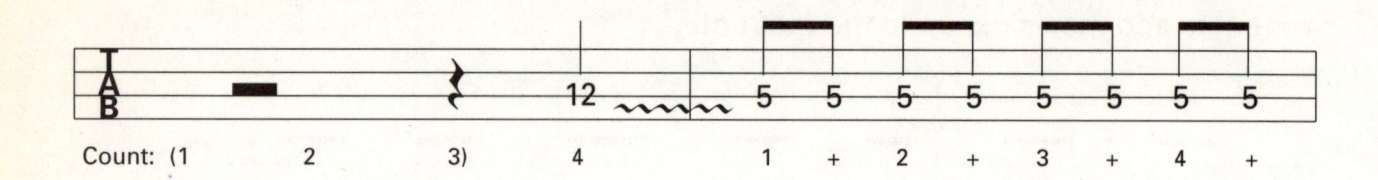

One more way of using slides is the addition of other chord tones.

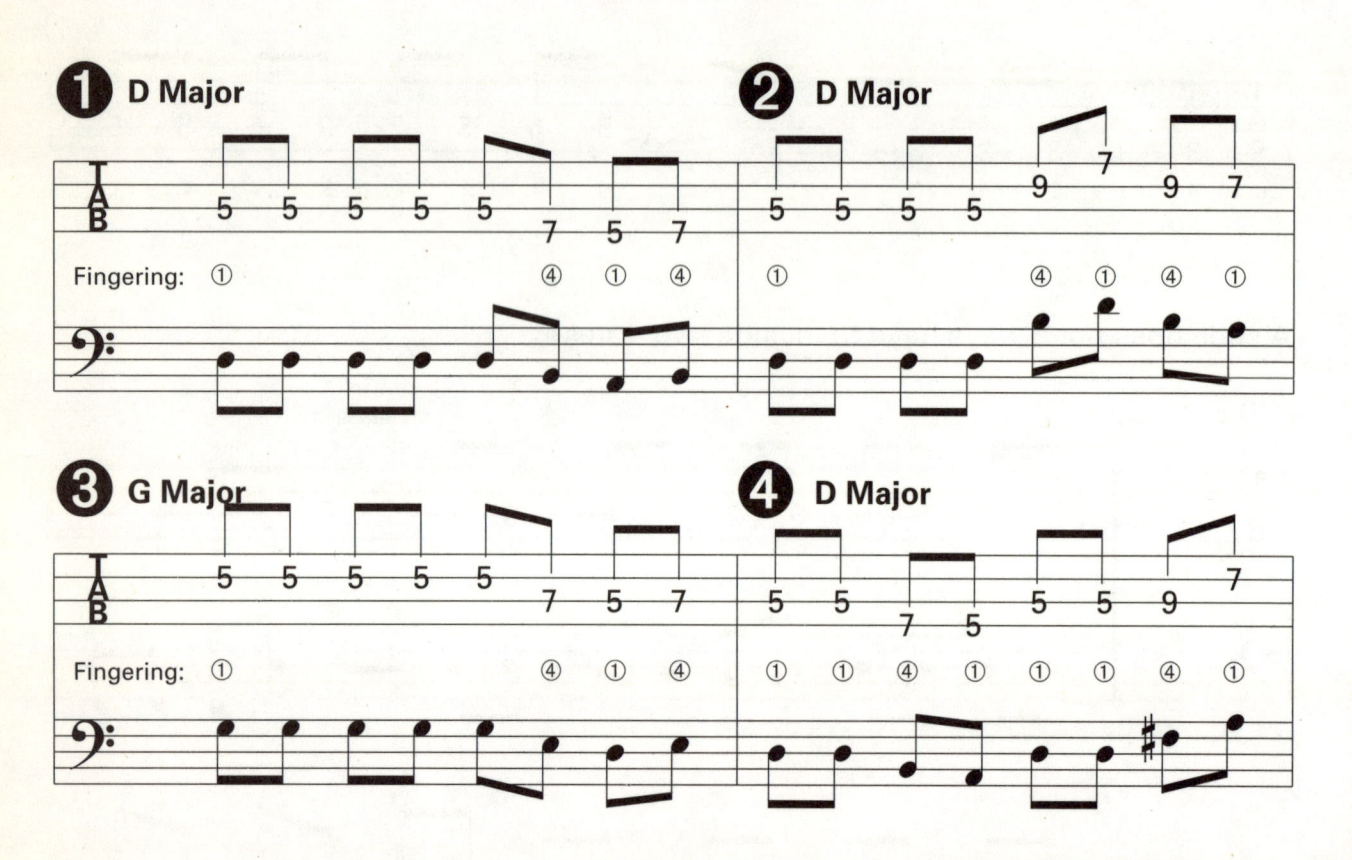

In bar 2 + 4 you can work in slides as well. Make them shorter this time:

Classical Pop

In the context of Pop productions influenced by Classical music, the E-bass often takes up the function of the tuba. Play the notes staccato, in order to get as close as possible to the sound of this instrument.
The added slides make this bass line even more interesting and should be played legato.

TAKE 36

TAKE 37

Bending Notes

Bending notes by applying half steps are often used in order to combine two different chords, or are used within chords.

TAKE 38

"Double stops" are becoming more and more popular in Rock and Pop music. Double stops means playing two notes at the same time.

Double Stops in 10ths

TAKE 39

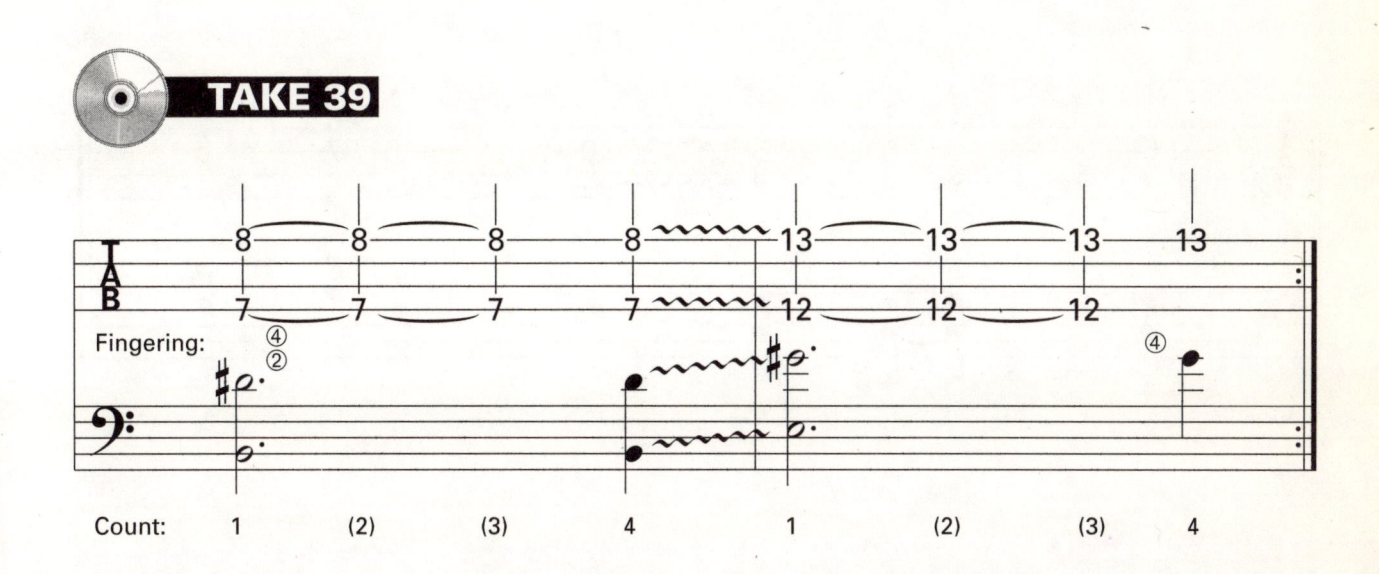

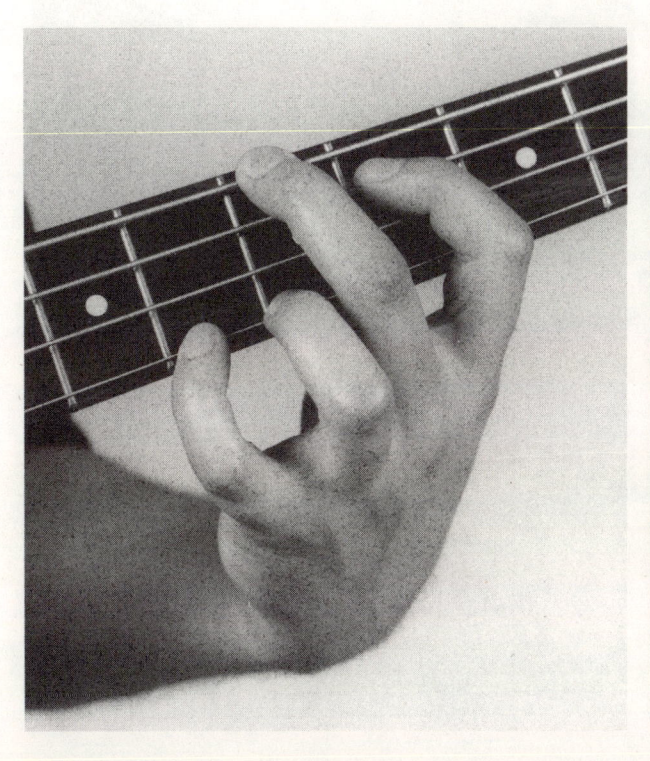

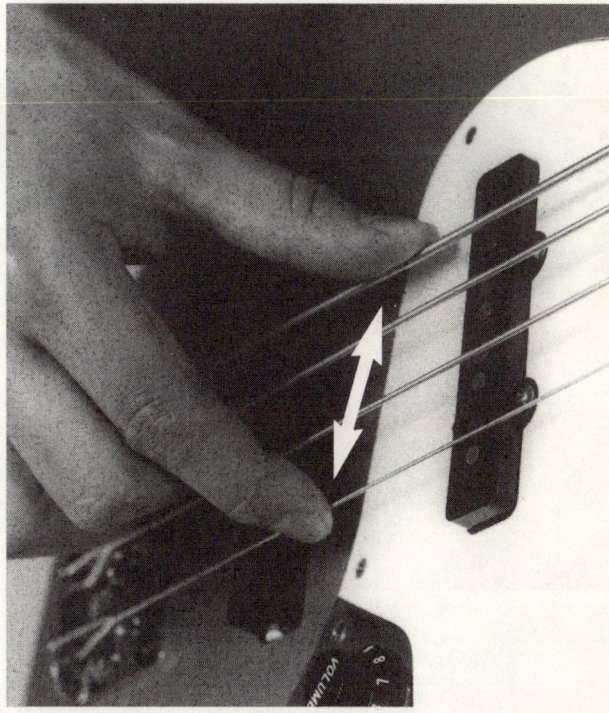

Double Stops in 5ths

TAKE 40

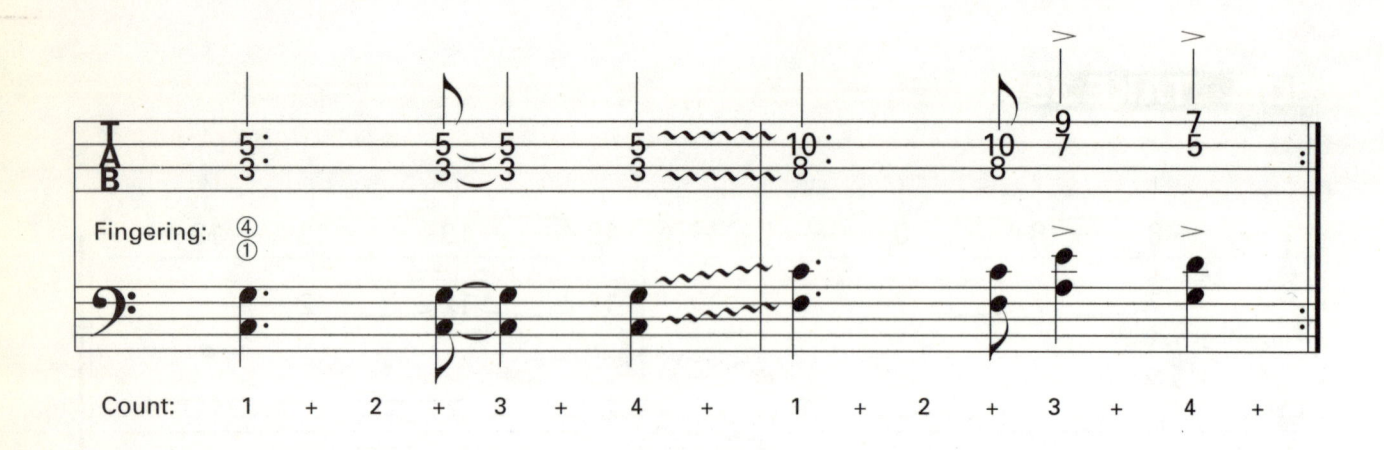

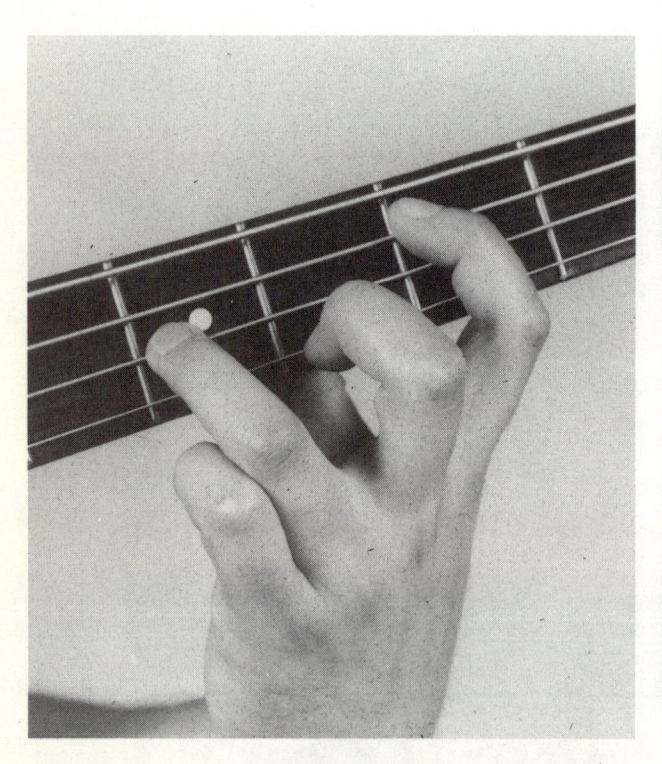

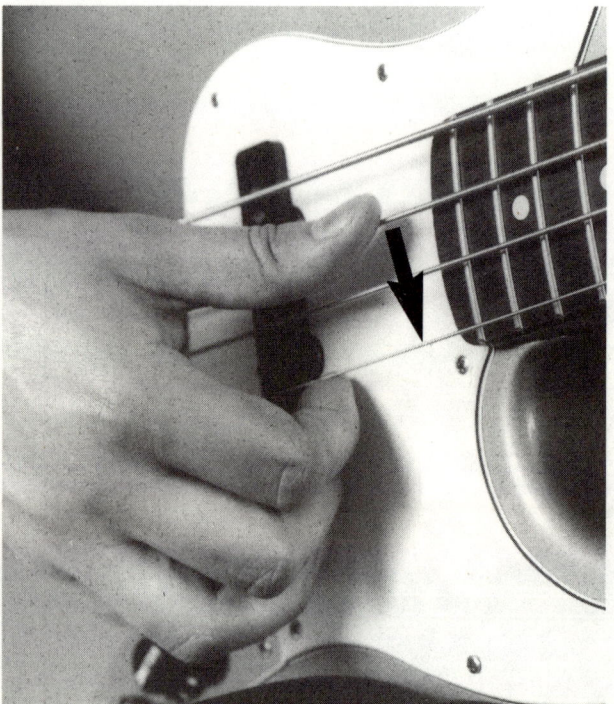

One more time: 5th intervals and single notes.

TAKE 41

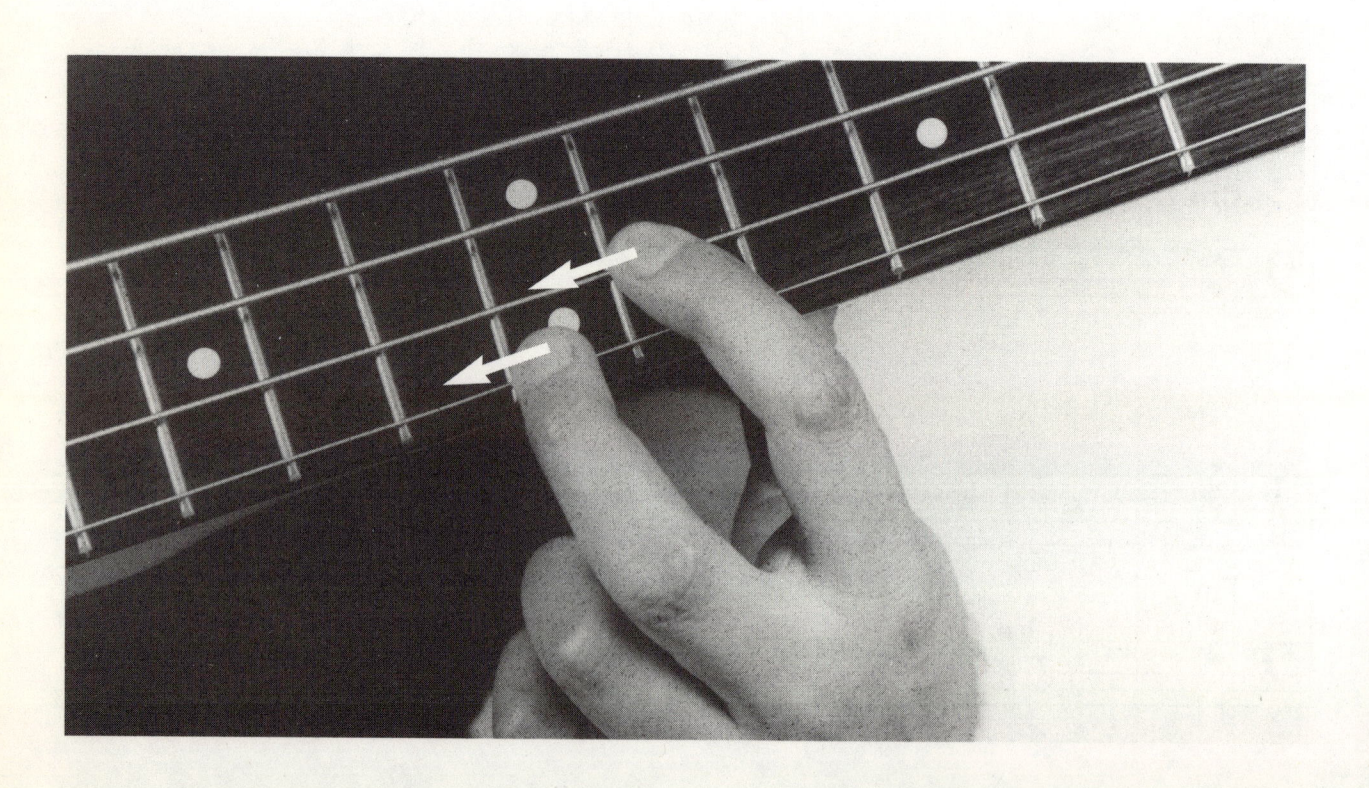

Double Stops in Major 7ths

TAKE 42

Double Stops in Minor 7ths

TAKE 43

Funk is Fun

The following bass lines are good practice for getting into the sixteenth-note subject. Here are the "normal" eighth notes:

[1/8 notation example]

In 16th-note notation, the bass line transcribed above looks like this:

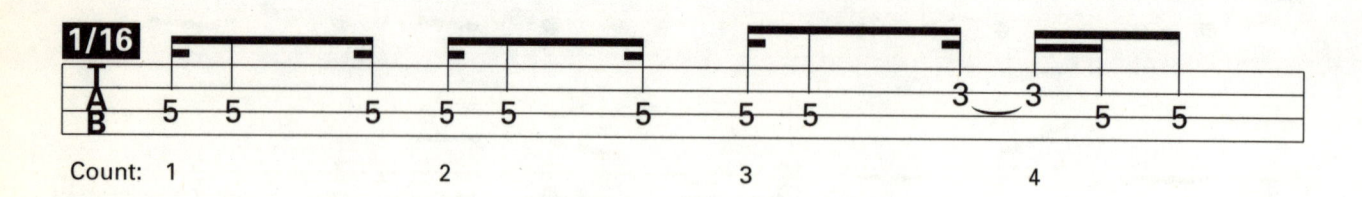

[1/16 notation example]

Both bass lines are identical, only the notation is different. At a constant tempo, it ought to be played twice as fast. Another example:

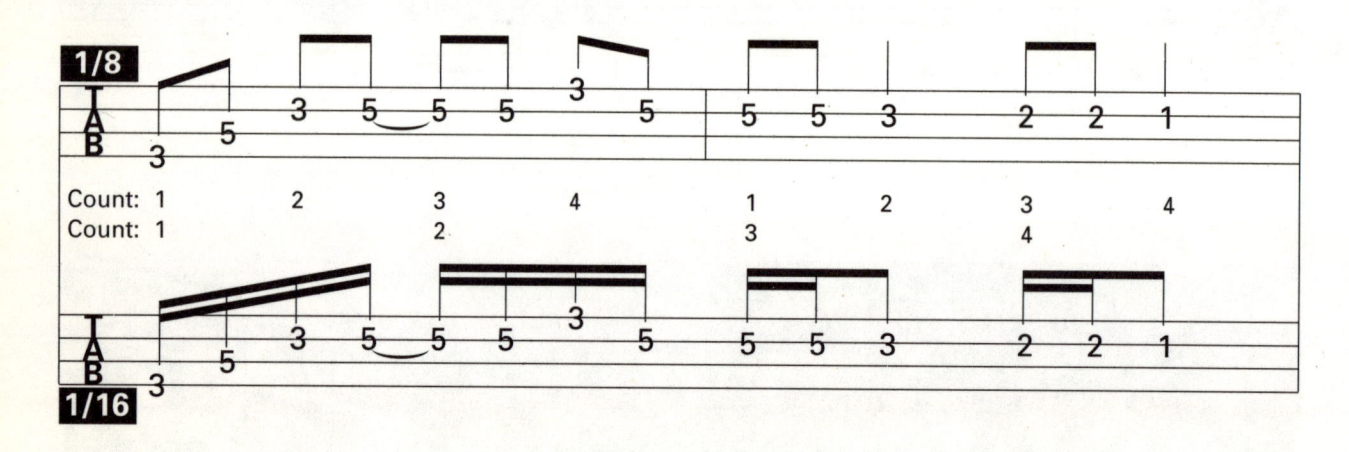

[1/8 and 1/16 notation example]

You see it's the same bass line, played once in normal (eighth) and then in double time.

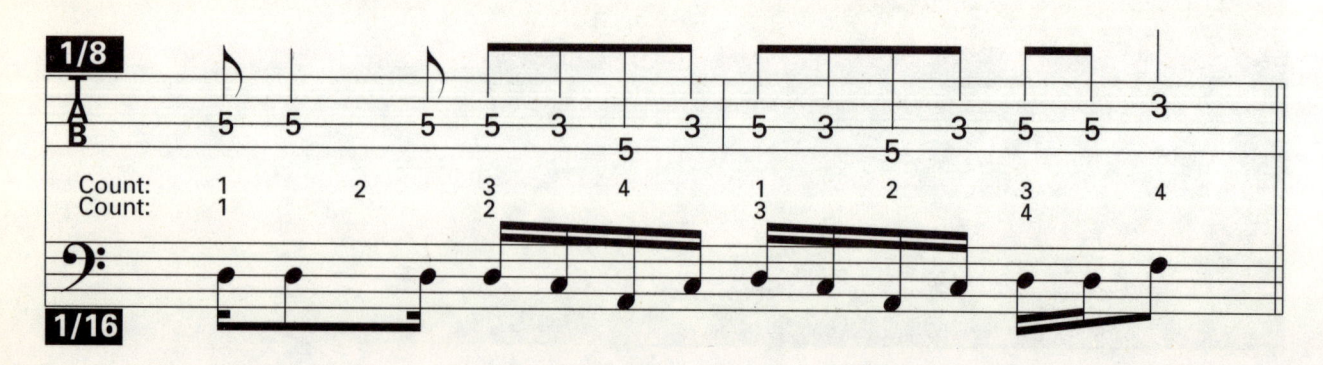

[1/8 and 1/16 notation example]

106

Count a 4/4 measure.

1- 2 - 3 - 4 - 1 - 2 - 3 - 4- and so forth

Now double the amount of notes (= eighth notes).

107

Fill-Ins (in 8ths + 16ths)

Fill-ins are used to combine musical phrases, e.g., from the first verse of a song to the second, or from the second verse to the chorus, or a solo part.
In the following piece, the first seven bars are given. In bar 8, you can create your own fill-in, before repeating the whole line.

Here are some possible fill-ins. But you will come up with great fill-ins yourself. Play the line again, always adding one of these fill-ins. Then play another one ...
Takes 44 - 57 always begin with bar 5 of the bass line on page 108 and then turn into fill-ins.

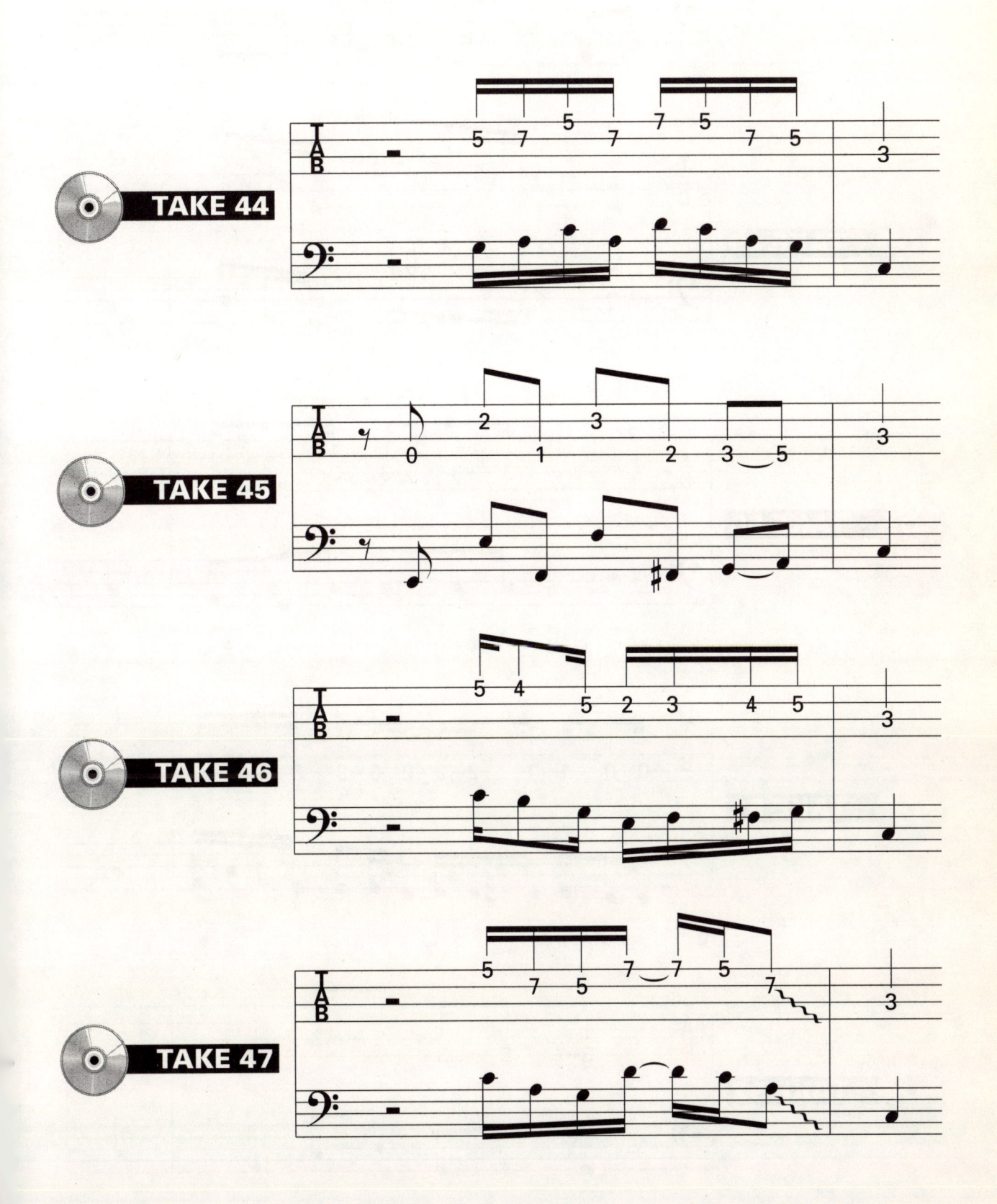

TAKE 44

TAKE 45

TAKE 46

TAKE 47

TAKE 48

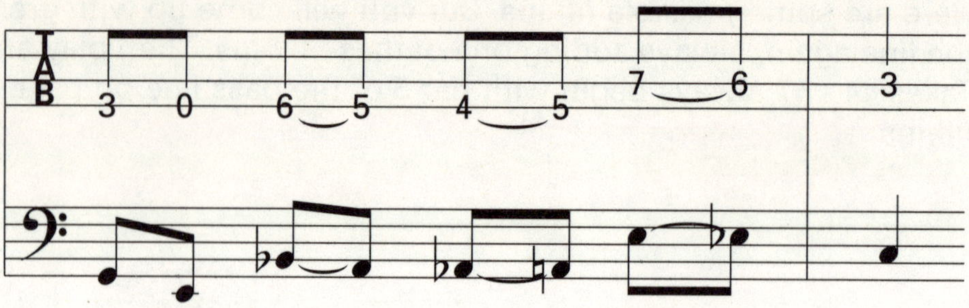

TAKE 49

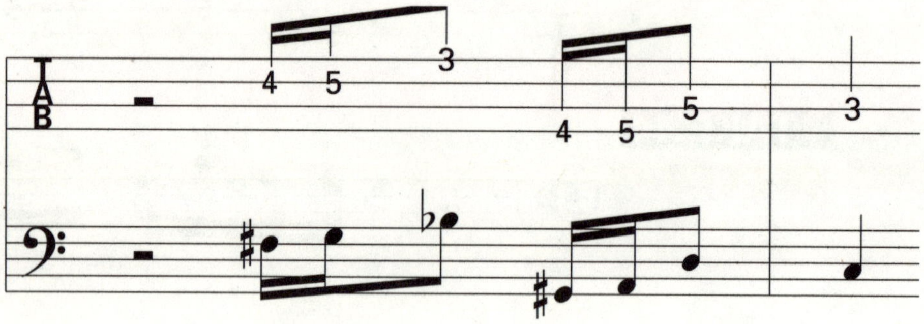

TAKE 50

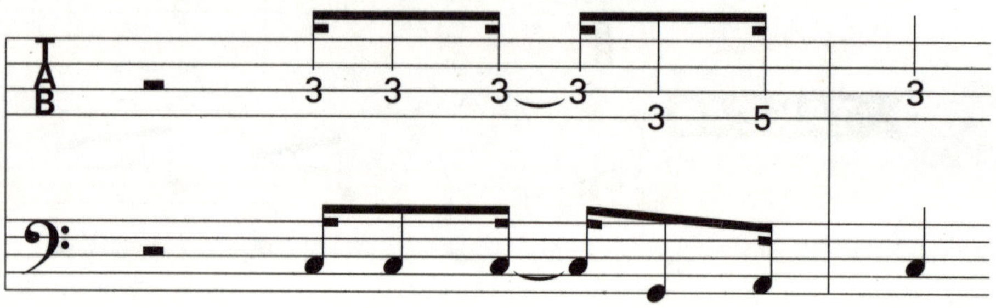

TAKE 51

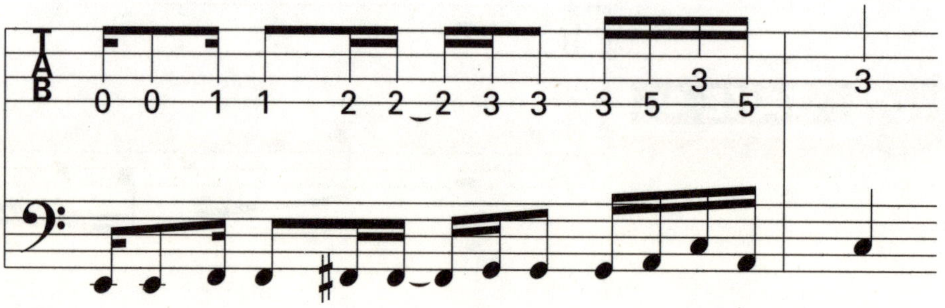

TAKE 52

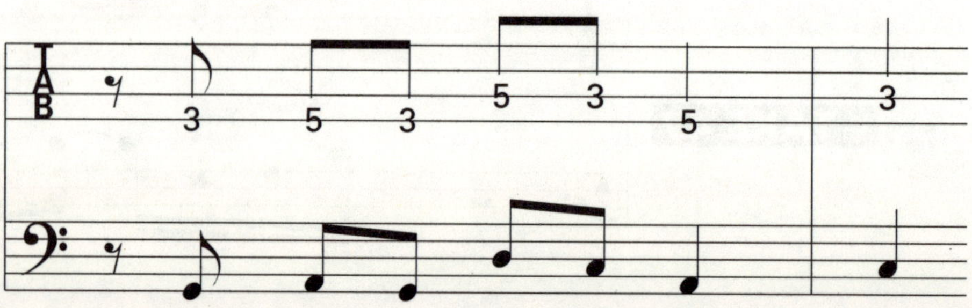

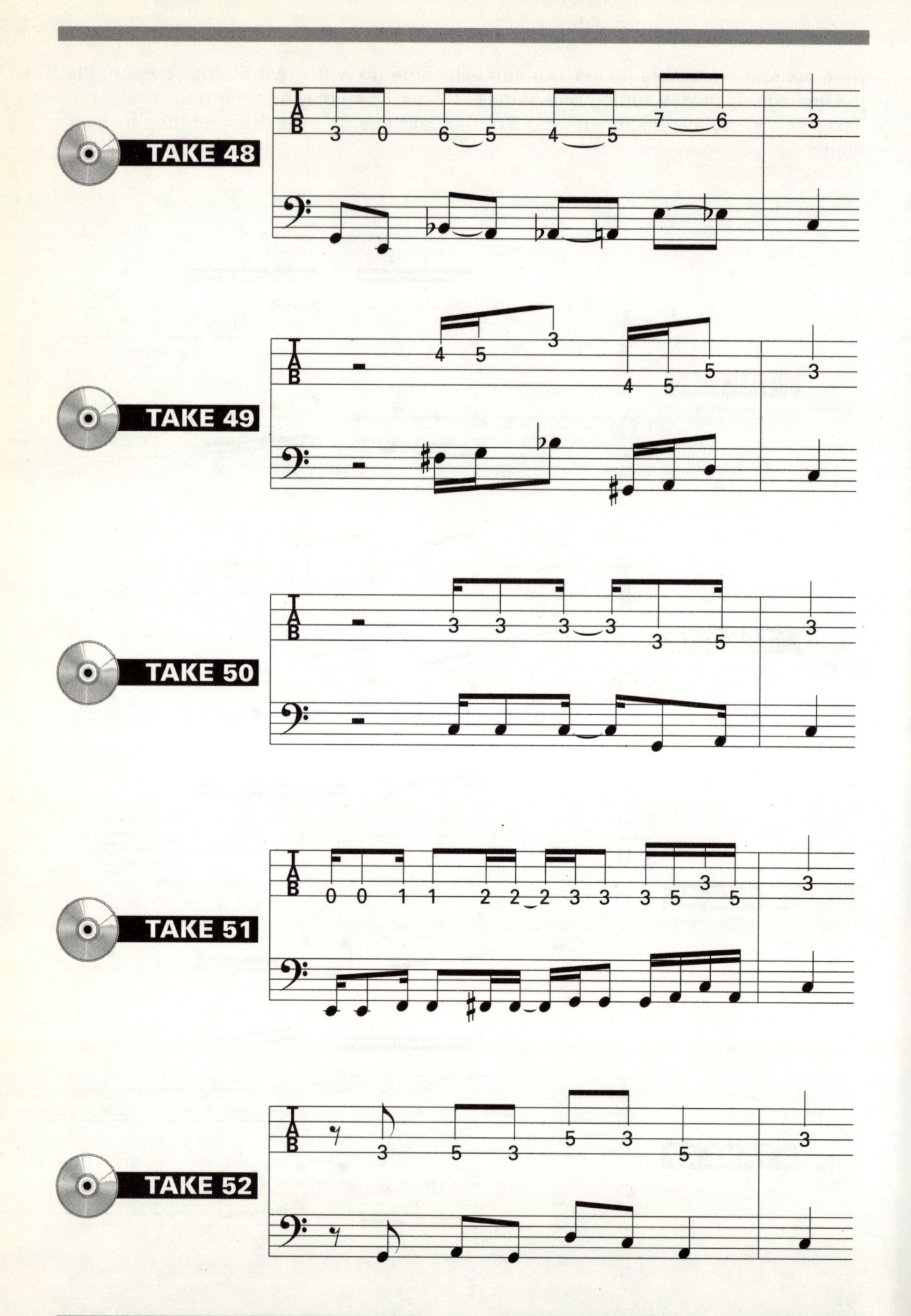

TAKE 53

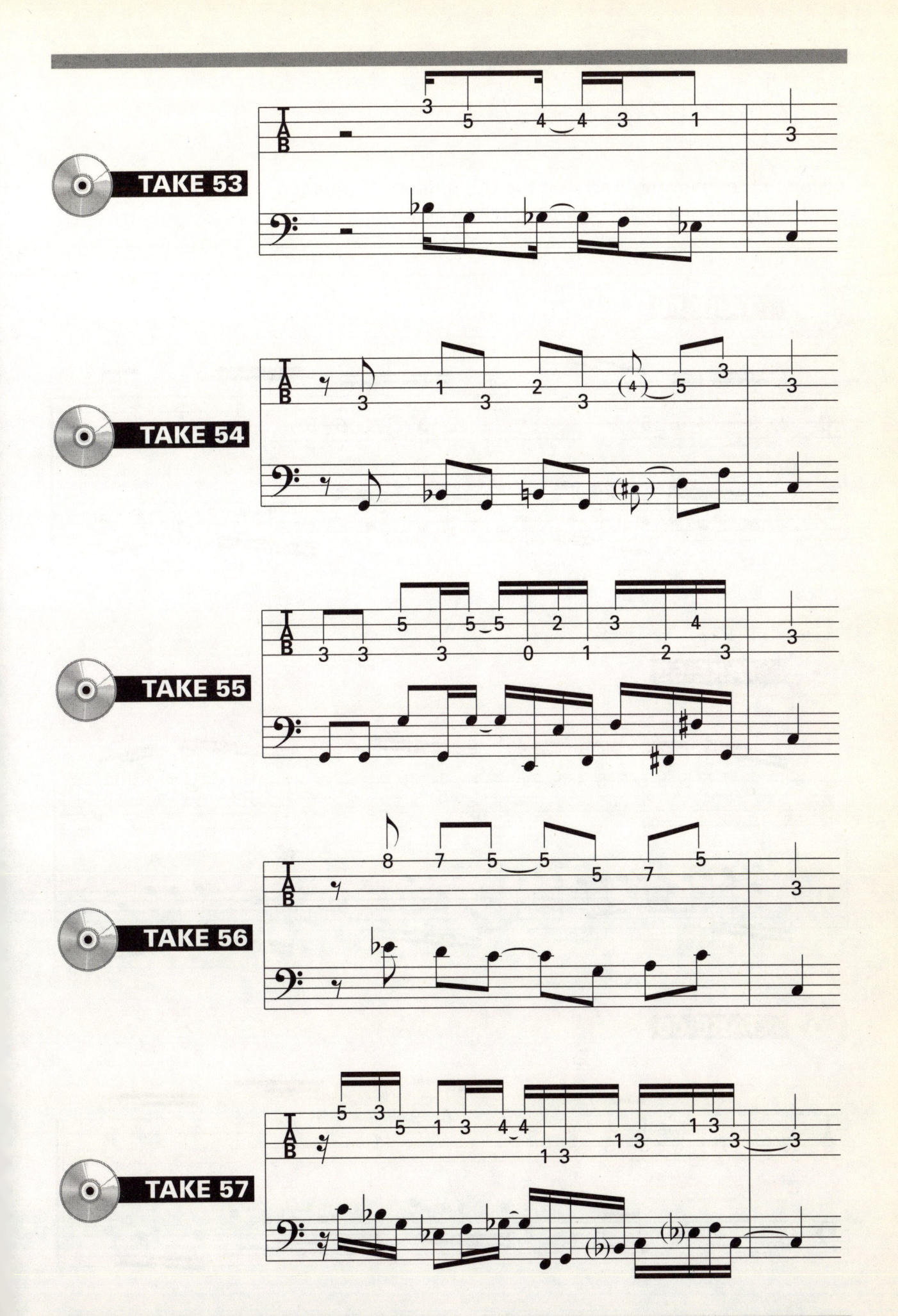

TAKE 54

TAKE 55

TAKE 56

TAKE 57

Fun(k) Licks

Listen to the following tracks on the CD, until it's "ringing in your ears" and you can read along without problems. Then play along:

TAKE 58

TAKE 59

TAKE 60

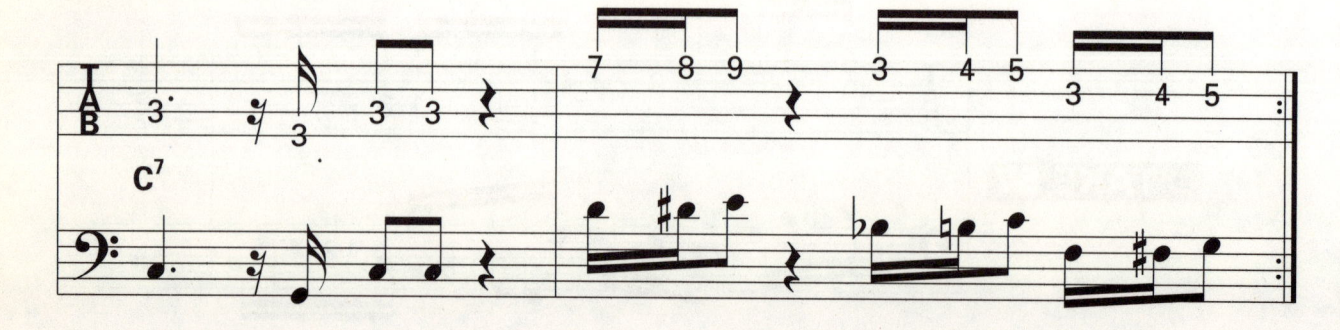

TAKE 61

More Funk

Make sure you don't miss the repeat signs, i.e., again and again, and again and...

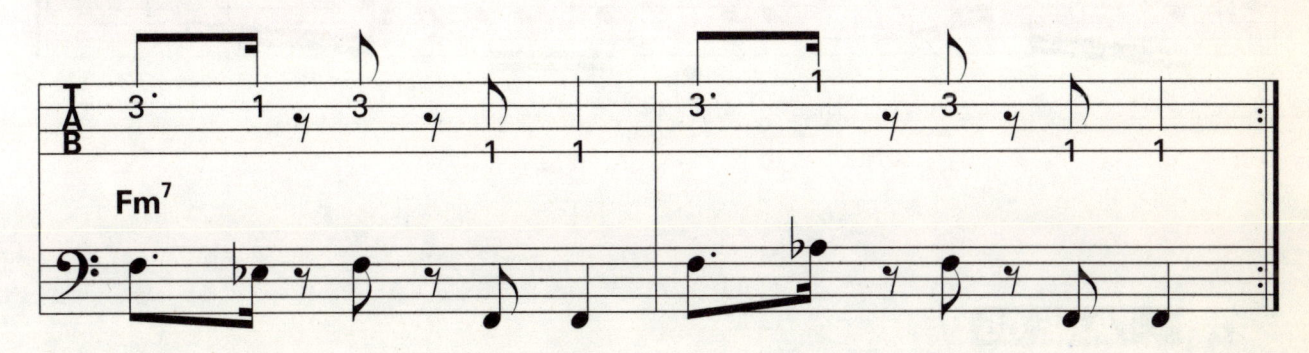

TAKE 62

TAKE 63

TAKE 64

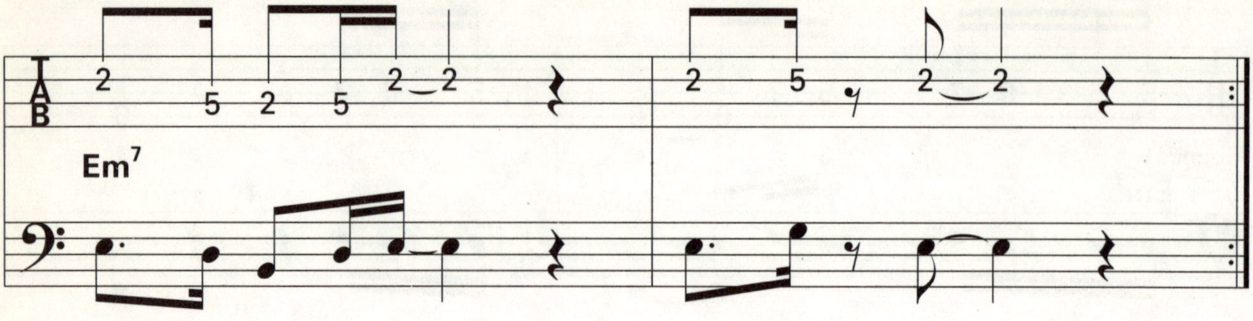

TAKE 65

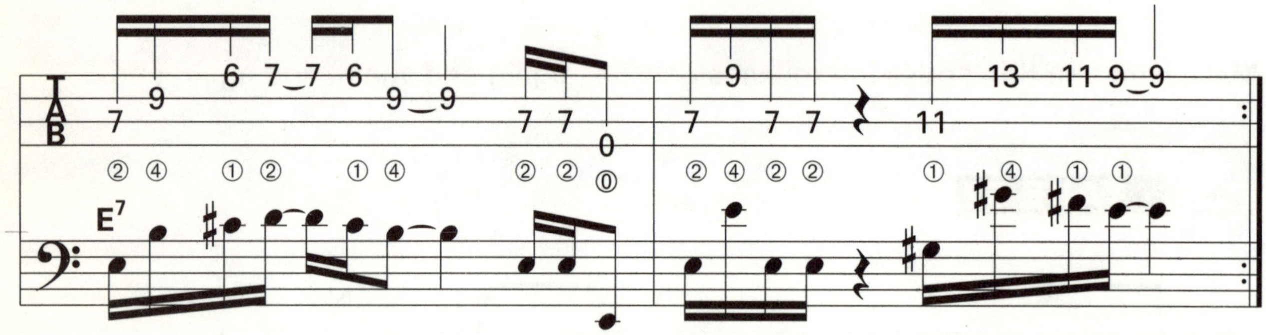

TAKE 66

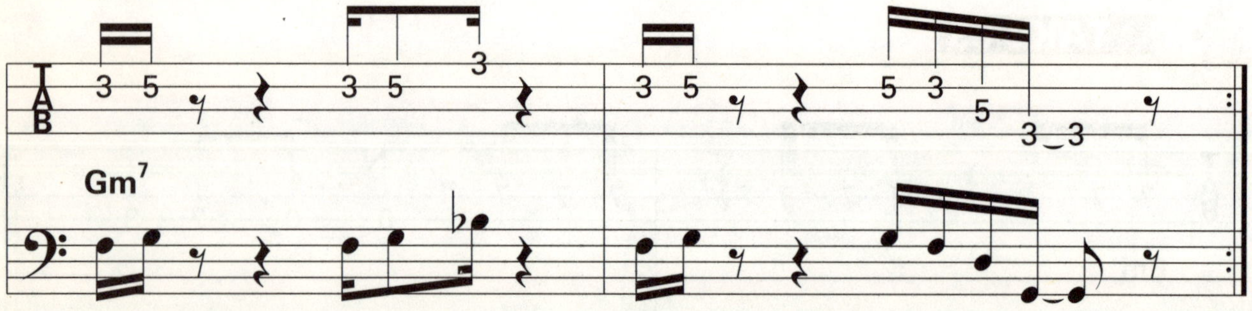

TAKE 67

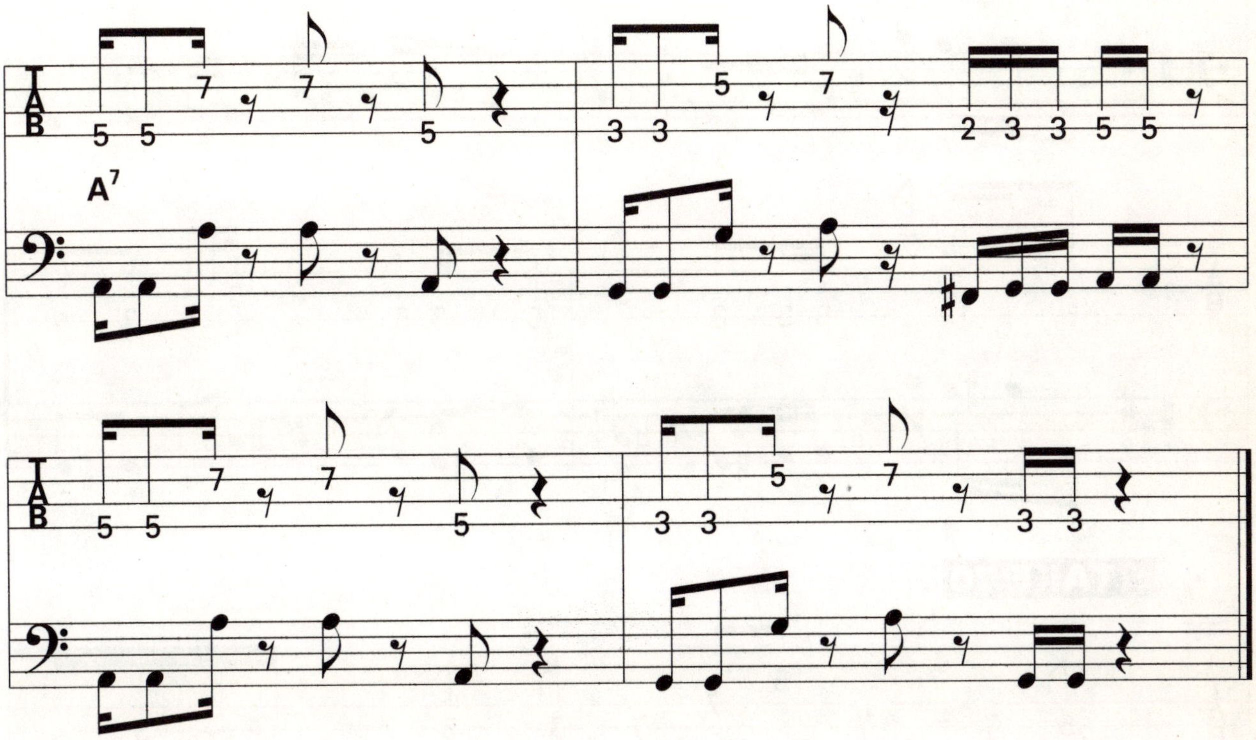

TAKE 68

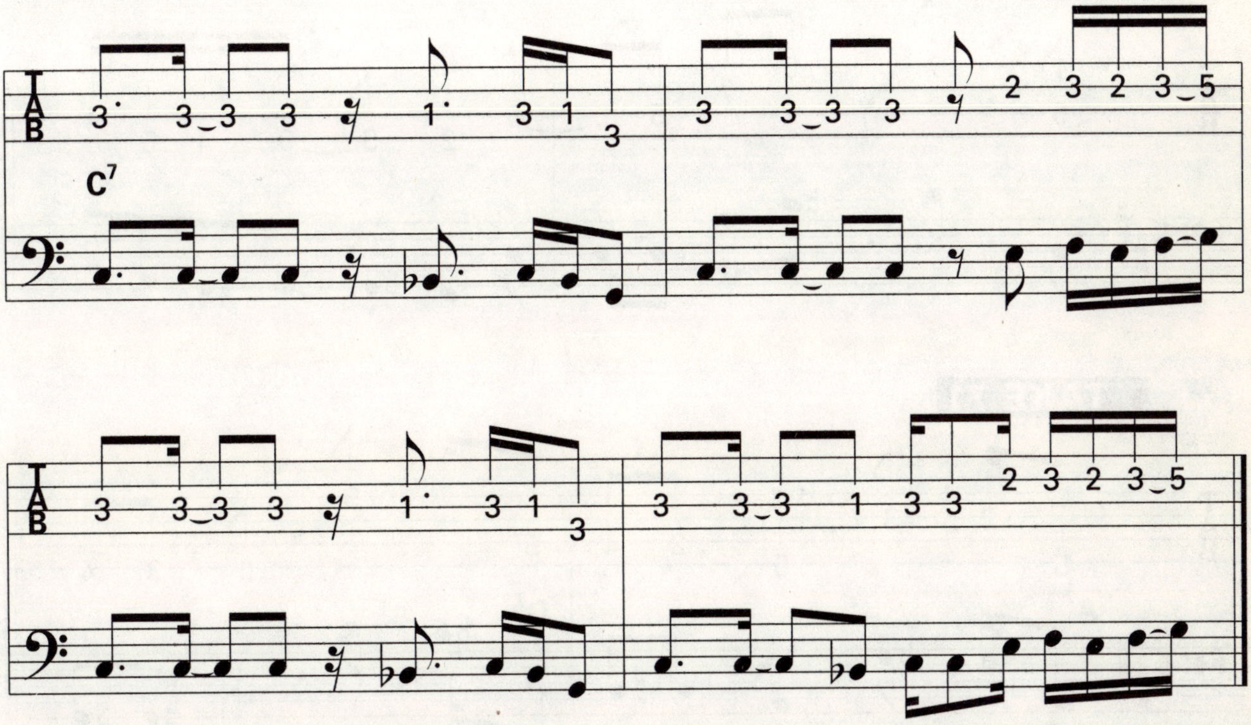

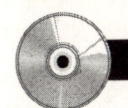

TAKE 69

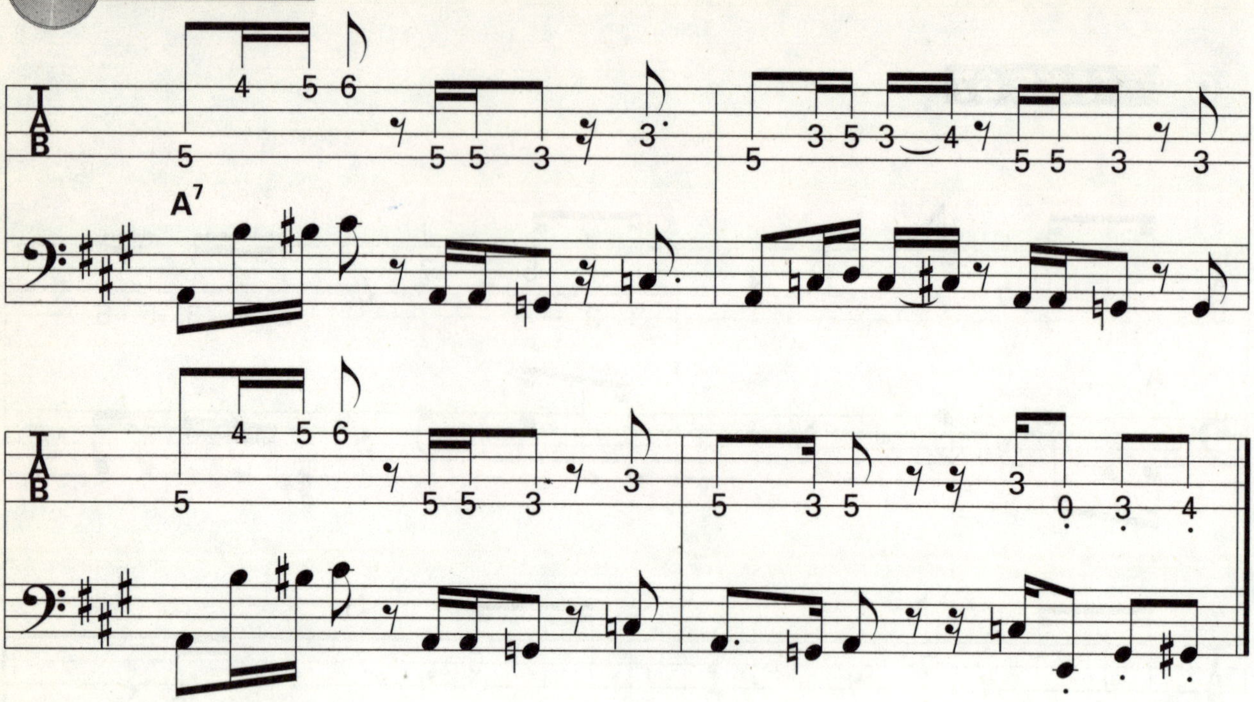

TAKE 70

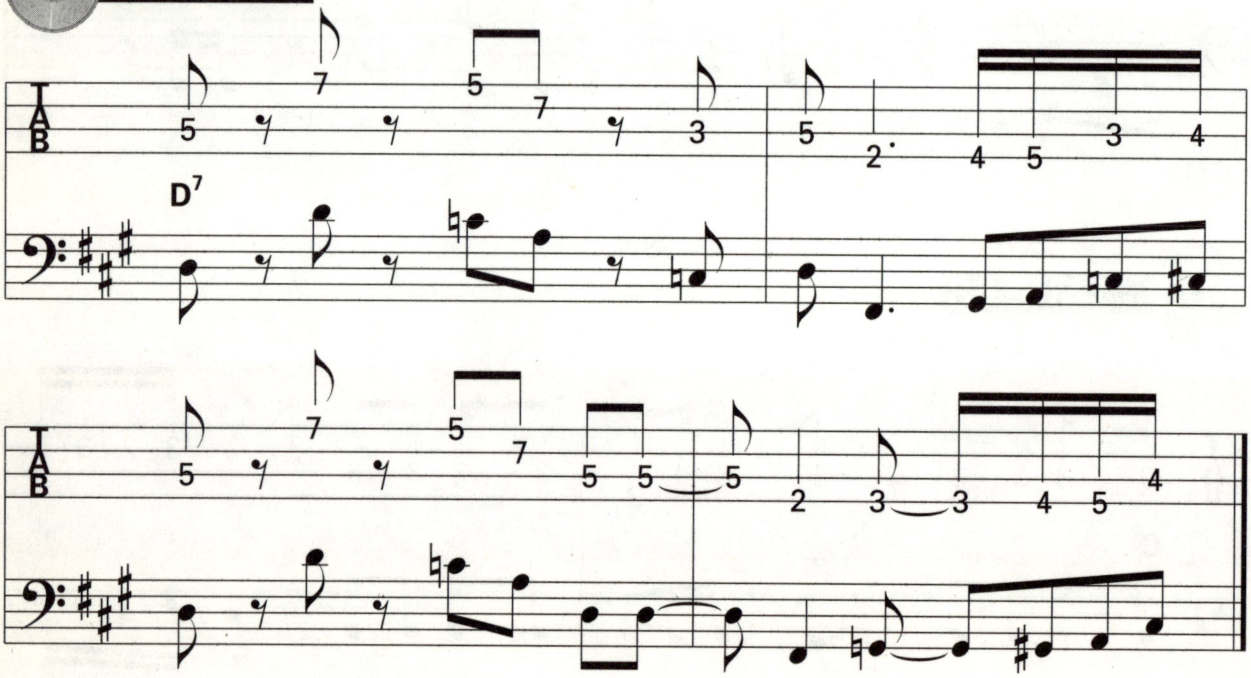

TAKE 71

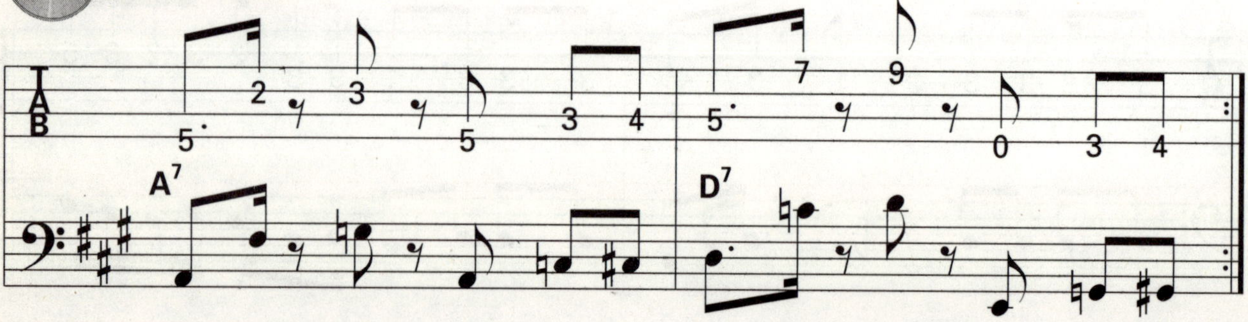

Motown Shuffle 1

Motown Shuffle 2

Motown Shuffle 3

Motown Shuffle 4

TAKE 73

Rastaman Reggae

More Reggae

TAKE 76

123

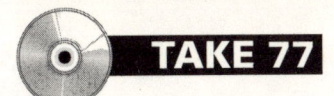

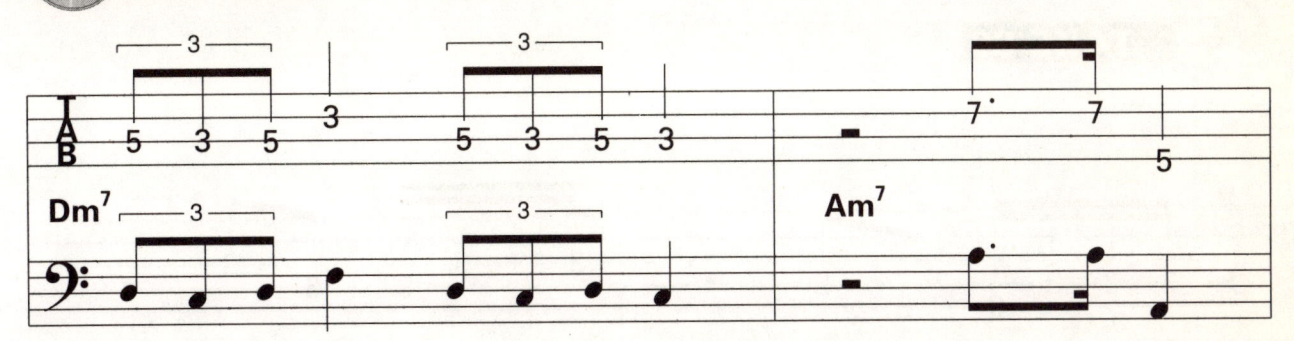

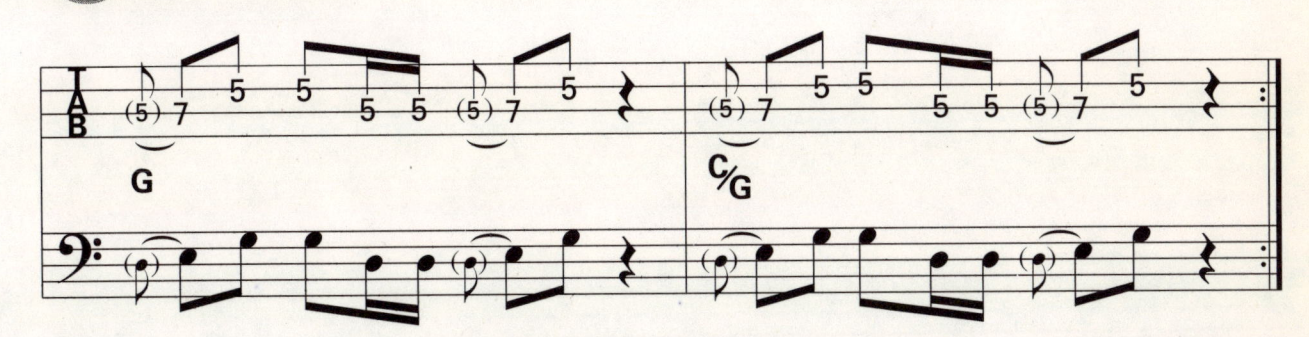

TAKE 80

Chapter 6

The Slap Bass Technique

This way of playing bass has become an established way of playing bass guitar in many styles of popular music. It is actually not as difficult as it looks. A few exercises will help you enrich your bass licks with this interesting technique.

One essential condition are well-balanced strings. Round-wounds or half-rounds are best suited for "slapping". They sound clearer and more precise than flat-wound strings.
Generally, the flexibility of the strings has nothing to do with their thickness, but with how tightly they are coiled and the material they are made of. I do not recommend buying a set of strings that are too light, because they tend to break easily. Your best bet is to go and try out several sets, and coordinate them with the rest of your equipment (bass and amp). If you still have difficulties finding a good balance, you can try to adjust the height of your pick-ups and thus fine-tune your sound. As this way of playing bass produces a great deal of overtones, you can perfectly tune the sound by adjusting the magnets to the string.

The "slapping" technique features some positions which need further explanation.

The Thumb Stroke

The main difference to the common way of playing is the hand position and technique. The following photos show the most common starting position.

In the first picture, you can see the "snapped off" thumb. With the joint of your thumb sticking out, you strike the string loosely, somewhere close to the end of the fretboard. Doing this, your arm rests loosely at the edge of the body. Make sure you get the power for the action from your wrist and your arm rests in the same position. The other fingers hang loosely, close to the G-string, with the little finger supporting the hand from the body.

The technique described in example 2: The thumb is bent downward, with a little twist towards the inside. Decide yourself which of the two techniques your thumb likes best. Note how the index and middle fingers are positioned close to the D- and G-strings. With this way of holding your hand, you have an ideal starting position, not only for the downstroke but also for popping the upper strings.

Practice slapping on the E-string first.
In the following examples, I notated a T (like thumb) for each slapping note.

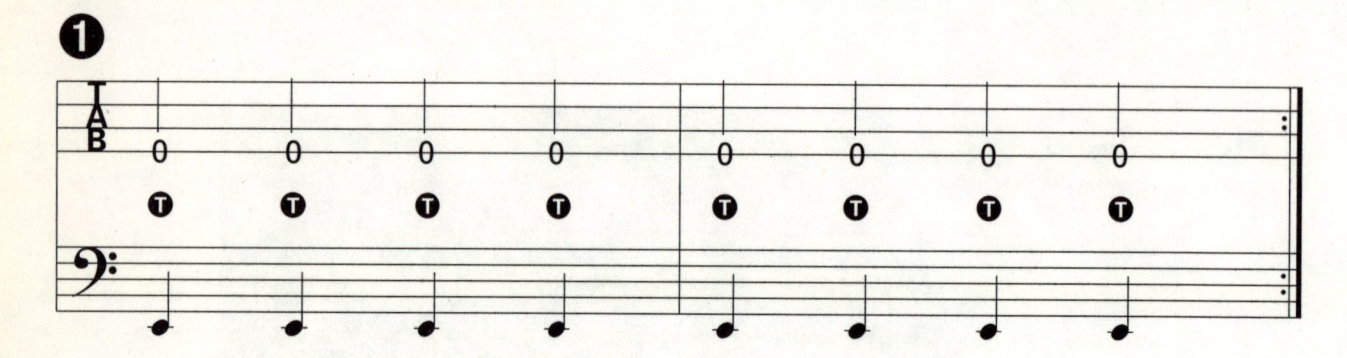

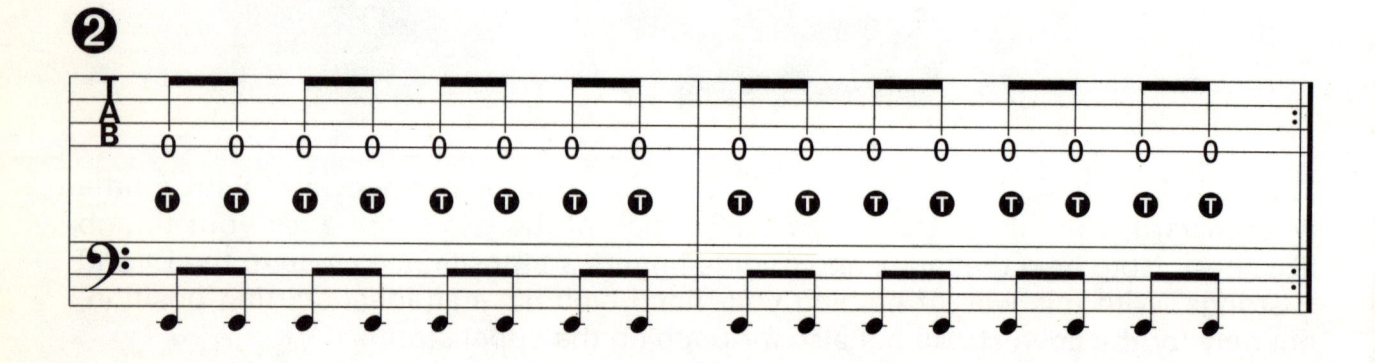

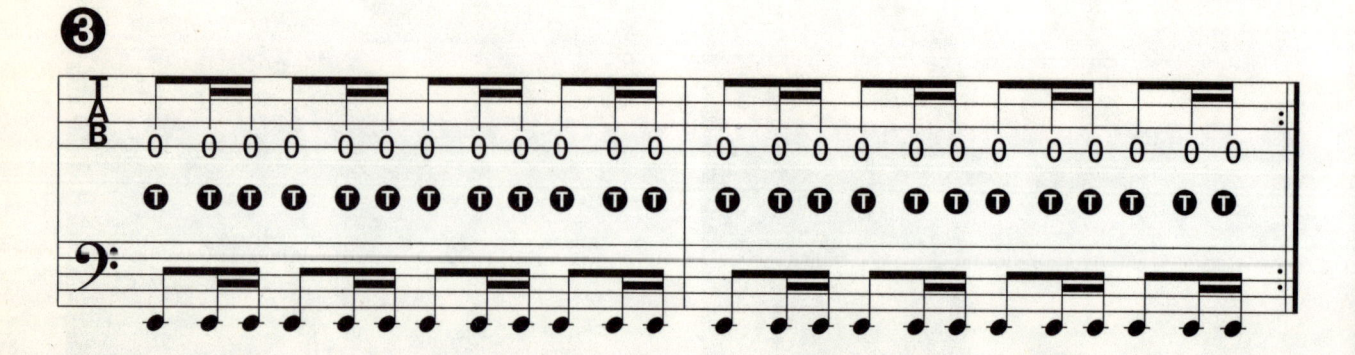

TAKE 81

❶

TAKE 82

❷

TAKE 83

❸

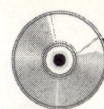

TAKE 84

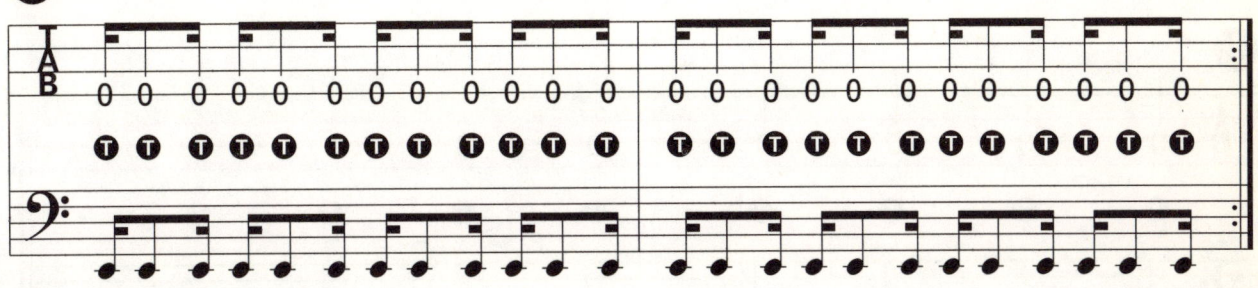

④

TAKE 85

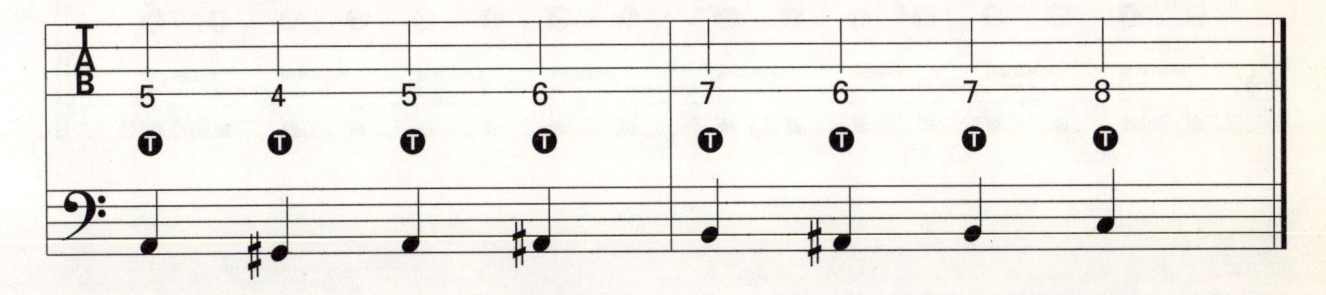

⑤

Here's the same thing on the A-string:

130

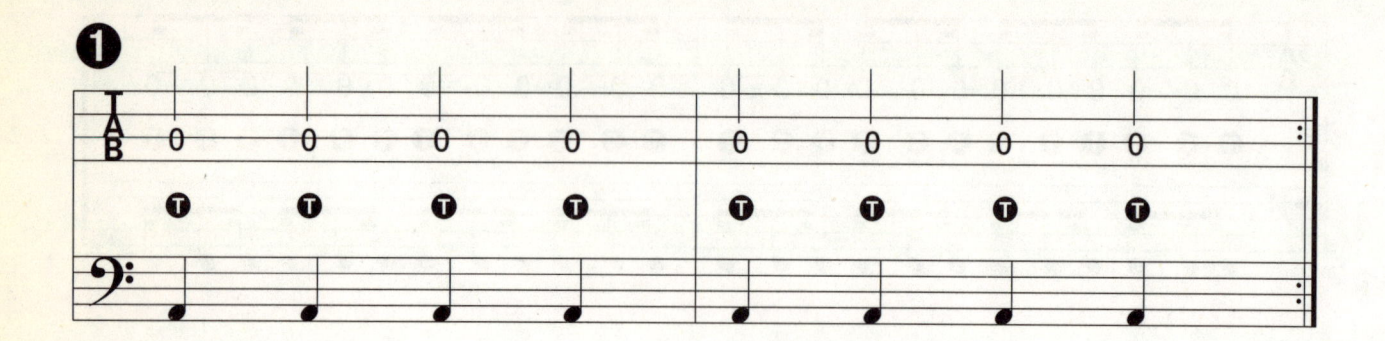

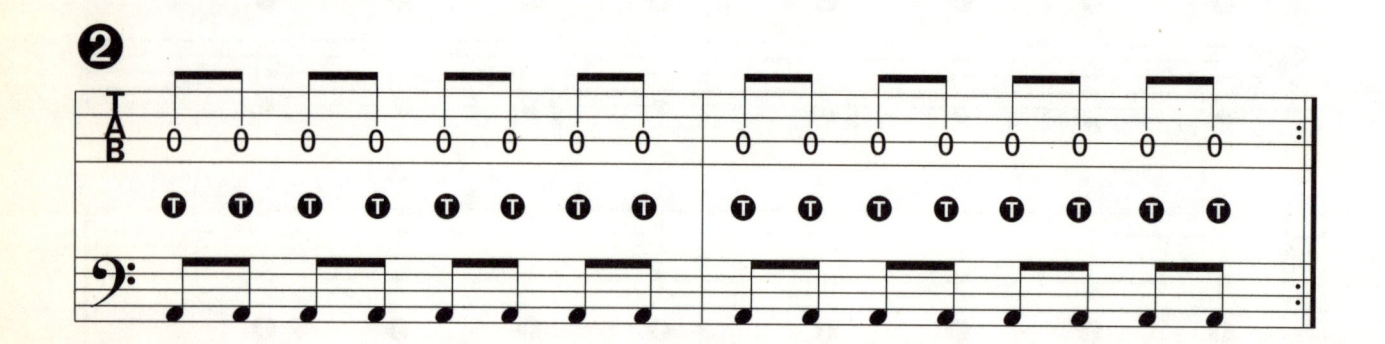

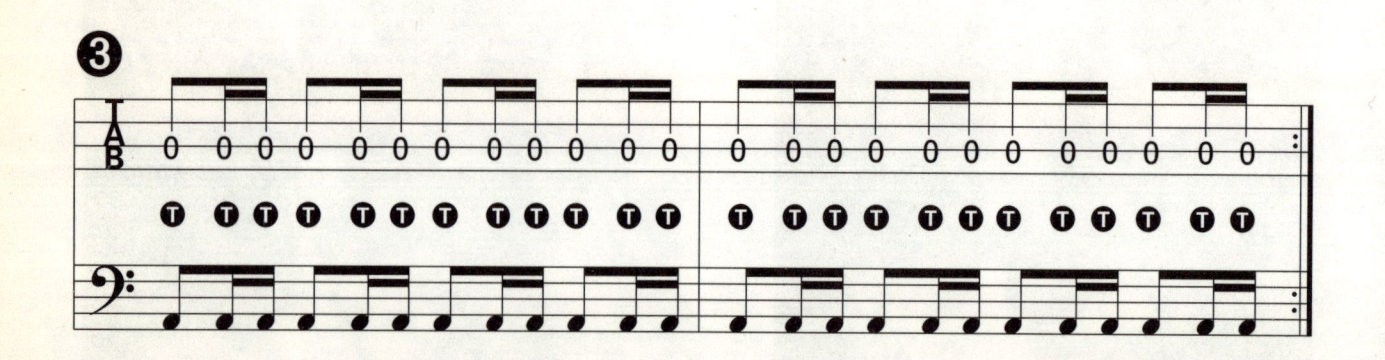

TAKE 89

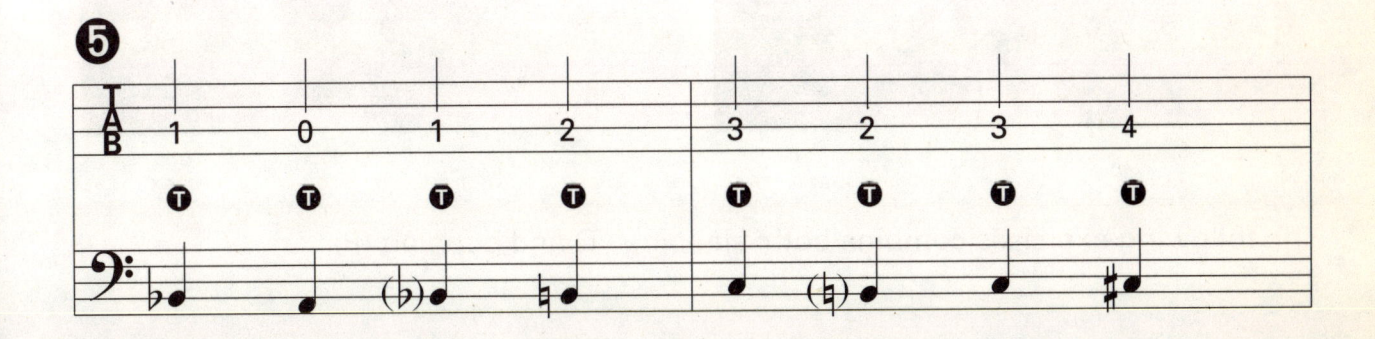

④

TAKE 90

⑤

String "Popping"

In order to pop the strings, you slide the tips of either your index or middle finger under the strings (not both of them!). Pop the string with as little of your fingertip as possible, in order not to pull it away from the bass.
You will soon develop a sense of how far to reach under the string to make it pop as hard as you want.

The following exercises combine both: slapping (T) and popping (P).

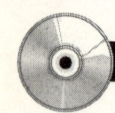

TAKE 91 (only variation 1)

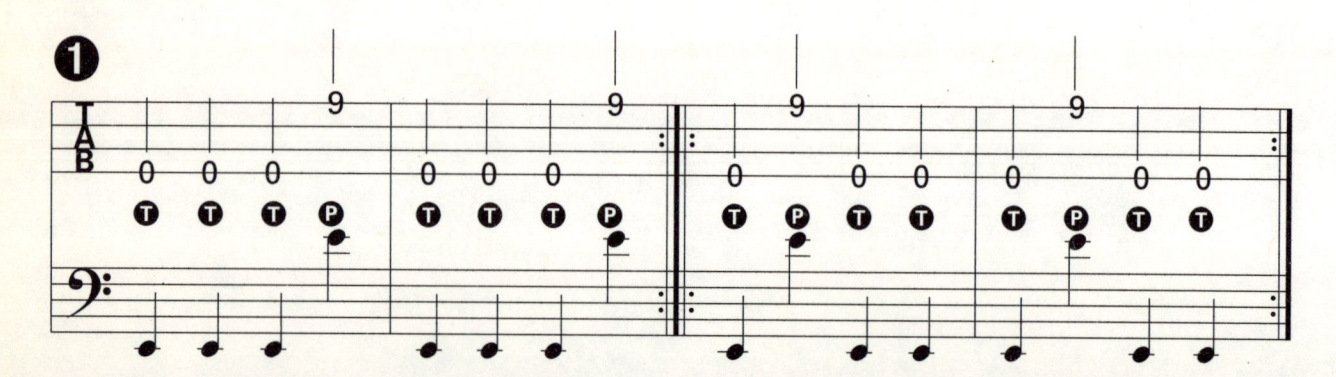

TAKE 92

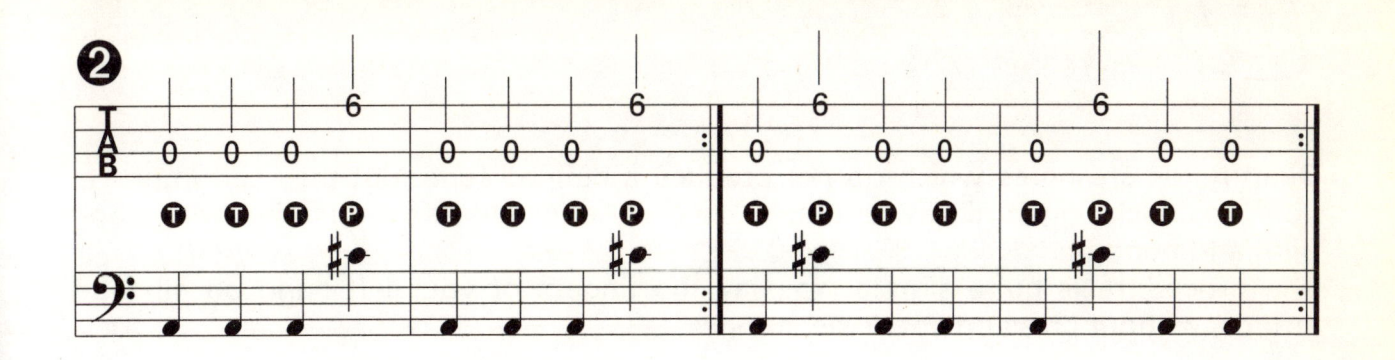

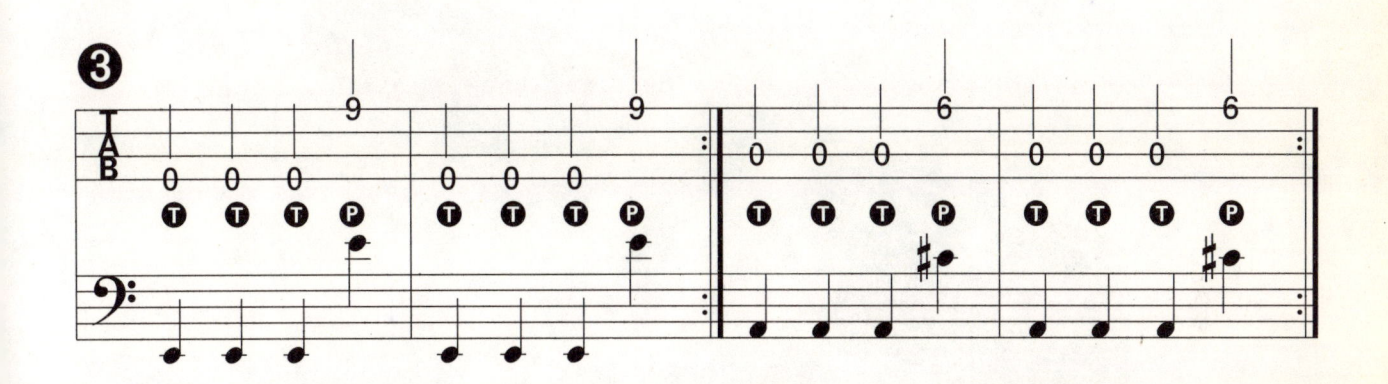

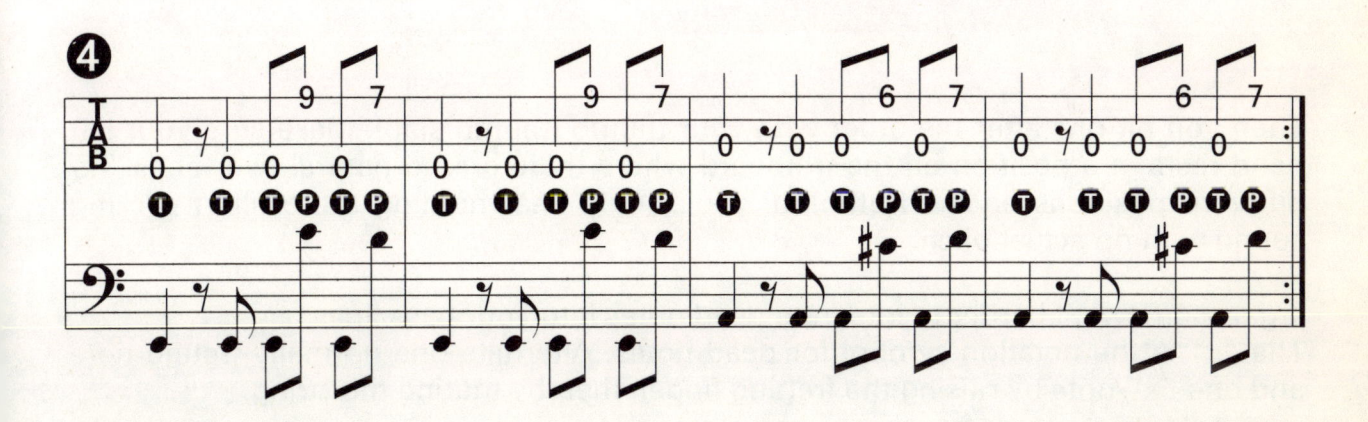

Dead Notes

Dead notes are notes which do not produce a defined tone. But they can improve your bass licks rhythmically, and are especially effective in combination with slapping and popping.
The procedure is quite simple. You lay the fingers of your left hand on all four strings, without pressing down the strings:

Then you hit one after the other with your thumb (thumb slap). Make sure your left hand rests in a position on the fretboard where there are no natural overtones. Try different positions on the fretboard; you should hear nothing but a short clicking sound with no actual pitch.

It gets somewhat harder to integrate dead notes into your bass lines.
The "x" is the notation symbol for dead notes. Alternate one normally fretted note and one "x"-note by raising the fretting finger, thereby muting the string.

As dead notes are mostly played on an open "deadened" string they are also notated on the open strings.

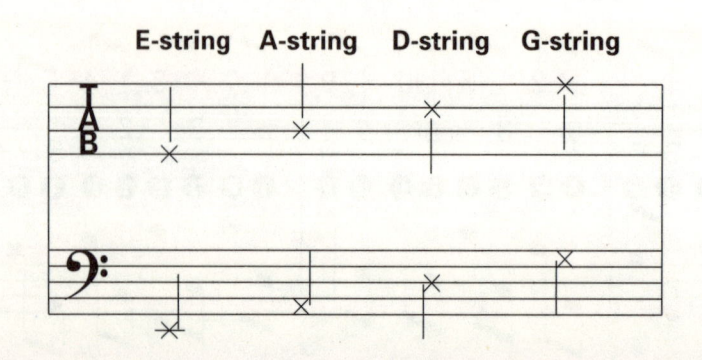

TAKE 93

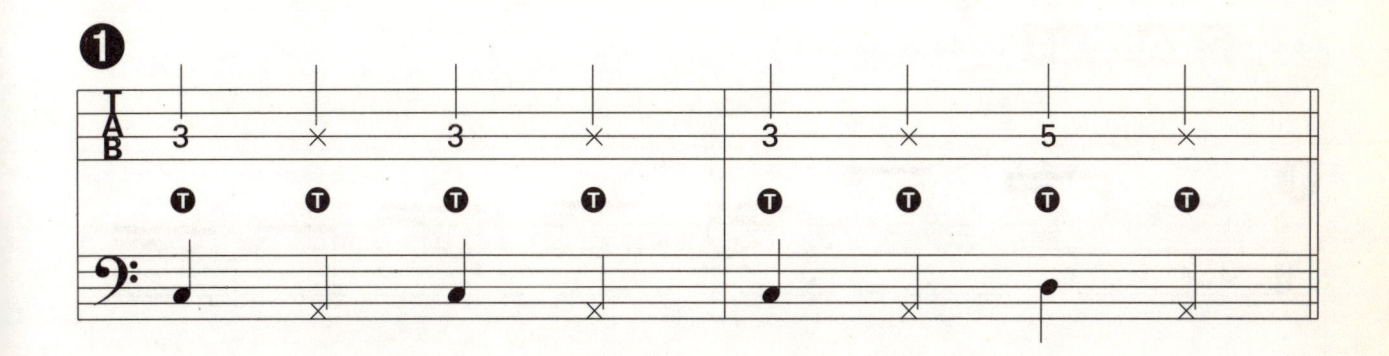

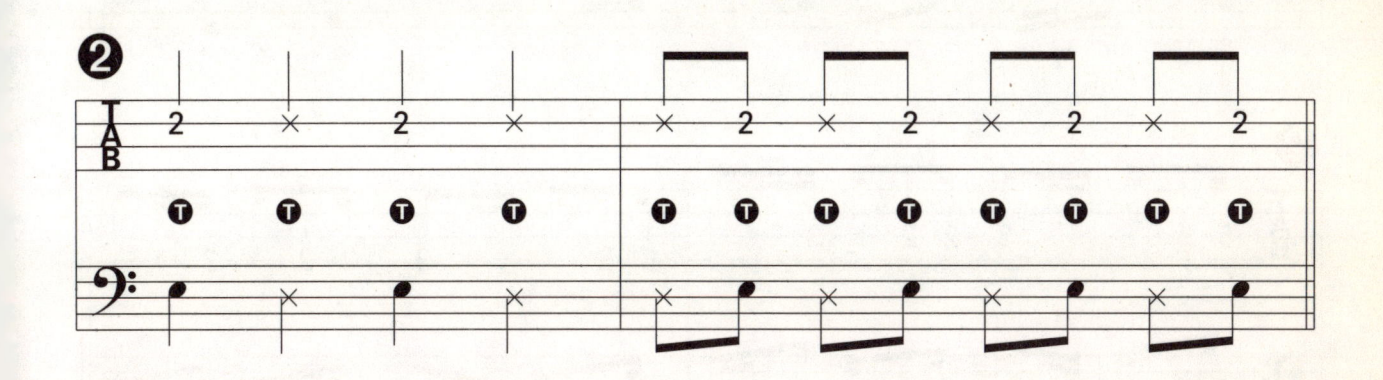

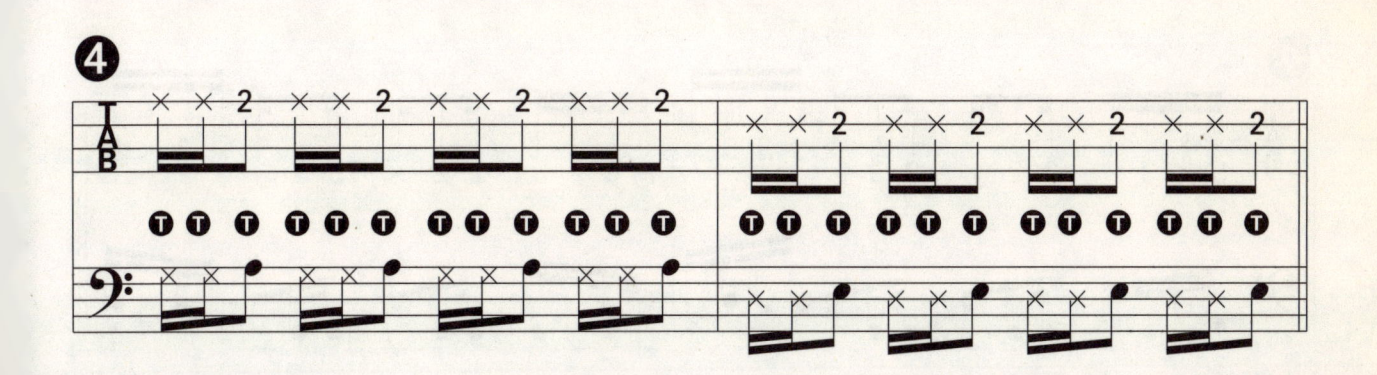

Try playing this exercise with a thumb stroke (thumb slap) and then use regular finger playing ...also pretty interesting!

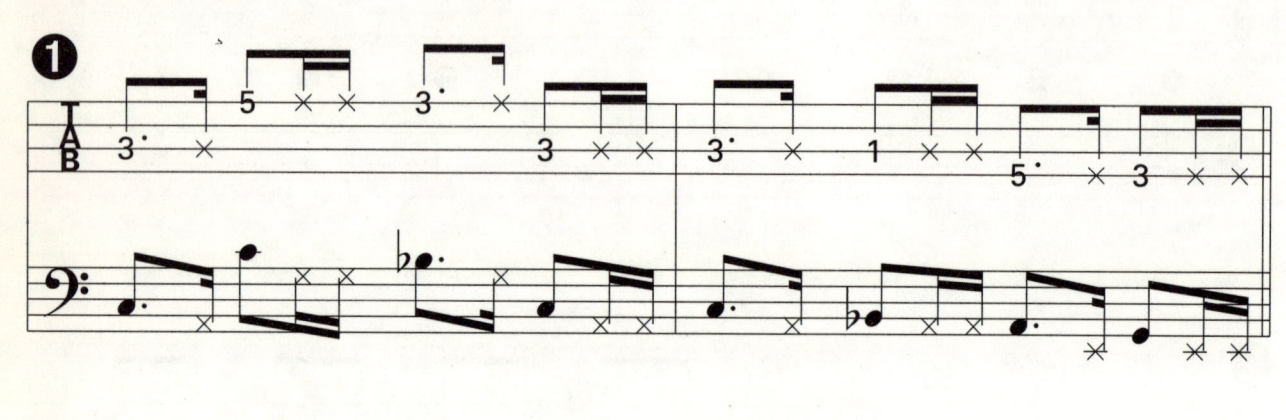

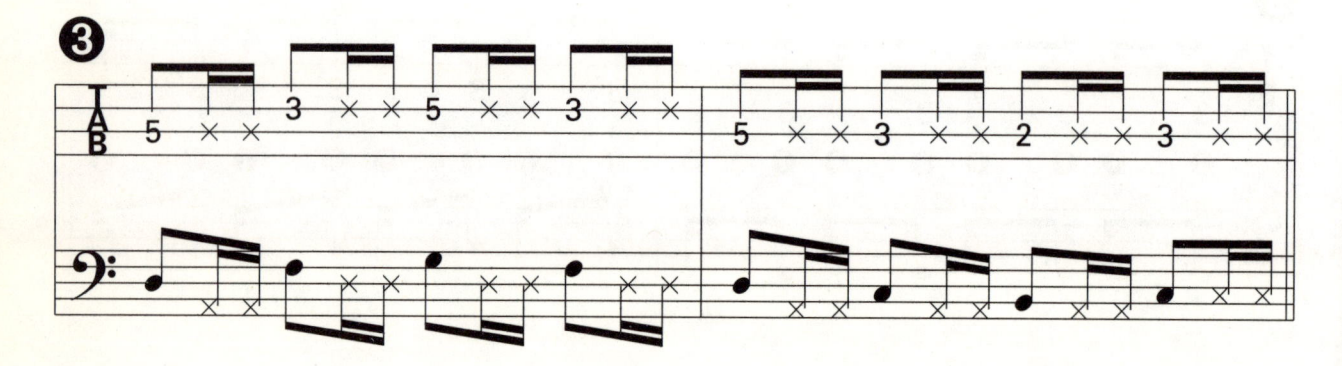

TAKE 94 (only variation 1)

Slap + Pop + Dead

The following exercises combine the previously covered playing techniques

TAKE 95 (only variation 1)

thumb stroke	popping	dead note
T	P	x

Hammer-Ons

...are really simple. You fret, for example, the "C" note on the A-string (with your index finger).

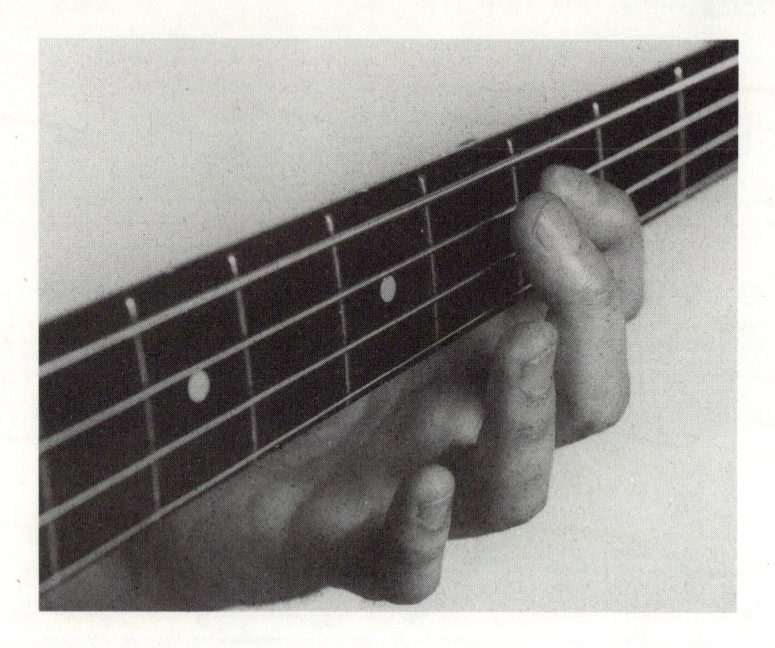

Hit the string either conventionally (finger picking ... index finger, middle finger, right hand) or with your thumb (thumb slap).

You play the next note "D" (also on the A-string) by "hammering" your left ring finger on the fretboard, making it sound, without having to hit the string again with your right hand. The index finger of your left hand remains in its original position (C, 3rd fret).

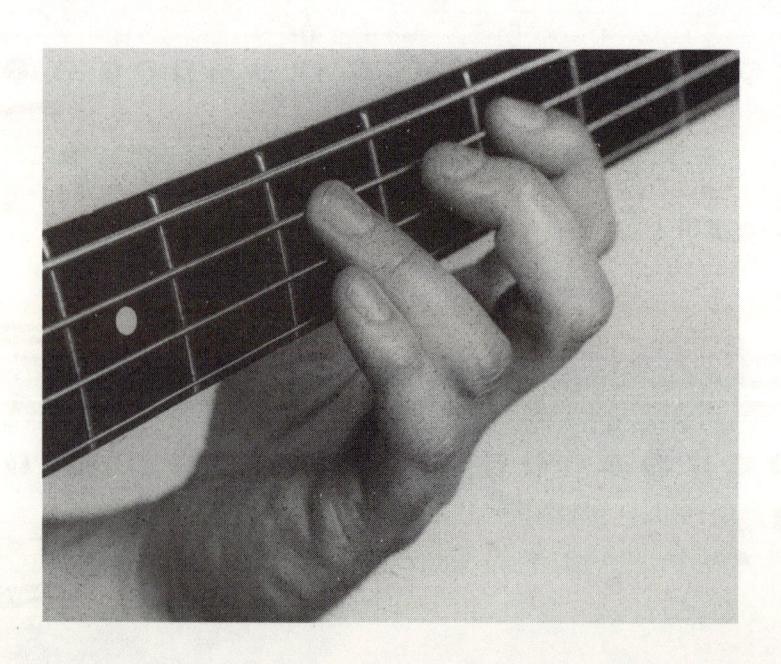

Here are some lines for you to check out (H/O) = Hammer-on)

TAKE 96

Pull-Offs

... are comparable to hammer-ons, only backwards. Play, for example, a "D" (A-string), which you fret with the ring finger of your left hand. At the same time, you fret the "C" note, which lies one whole step below the "D" (also on the A-string). After hitting the "D", you lift your ring finger and thus hear the (already fretted) note "C". All right?
For example:

(Pull-offs = P/O)

TAKE 97